I0813679

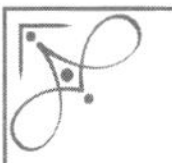

Presented To:

From:

Date:

As a Man Thinketh

soundwisdom

As a Man Thinketh

First published in 1903 by James Allen.

The Mastery of Destiny

First published in 1909 by James Allen.

The Path to Prosperity

First published in 1901 by James Allen.

Reprint edition by Sound Wisdom, 2025

This book is a historical artifact. Sound Wisdom has reprinted this work to preserve and share the best wisdom handed down from great men and women in history. Not all of the ideas and beliefs held by these authors remain acceptable in our present time, and Sound Wisdom does not condone or endorse every belief shared within this book. We encourage readers to glean the best timeless wisdom from these pages, while exercising grace toward our ancestors' flaws and forgiveness toward the mistakes of the past.

ISBN 13: 978-1-64095-132-7

Printed in China

1 2 3 4 5 6 7 8 / 29 28 27 26 25

Contents

As a Man Thinketh

The Mastery of Destiny

The Path of Prosperity

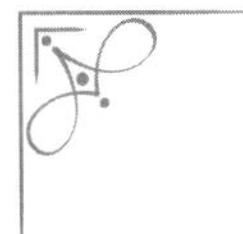

As a Man Thinketh

James Allen

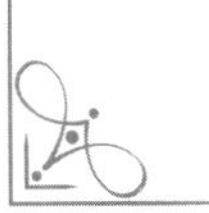
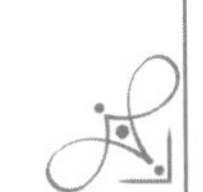

You will become as small as your controlling desire, as great as your dominant aspiration.

Foreword

This little volume, the result of meditation and experience, is not intended as an exhaustive treaty on the much written upon subject of the power of thought. It is suggestive rather than explanatory, its object being to stimulate men and women to the discovery and perception of the truth that they themselves are makers of themselves by virtue of the thoughts which they choose and encourage. That mind is the master-weaver, both of the inner garment of character and the outer garment of circumstance, and that as they may have hereto woven in ignorance and pain, they may now weave in enlightenment and happiness.

James Allen

CHAPTER 1

Thought and Character

As the plant springs from and could not be without the seed, so every act of a man springs from the hidden seeds of thought, and could not have appeared without them.

The aphorism, "As a man thinketh in his heart so is he," not only embraces the whole of a man's being, but is so comprehensive as to reach out to every condition and circumstance of his life. A man is literally what he thinks, his character being the complete sum of all his thoughts.

As the plant springs from and could not be without the seed, so every act of a man springs from the hidden seeds of thought, and could not have appeared without them. This applies equally to those acts called "spontaneous" and "unpremeditated" as to those which are deliberately executed.

Act is the blossom of thought, and joy and suffering are its fruits. Thus does a man garner in the sweet and bitter fruitage of his own husbandry.

Thought in the mind hath made us. What we are by thought was wrought and built. If a man's mind hath evil thoughts, pain comes on him as comes the wheel the ox behind. If one endure in purity of thought, joy follows him as his own shadow, sure.

Man is a growth by law, and not a creation by artifice, and cause and effect is as absolute and undeviating in the hidden realm of thought as in the world of visible and material things. A noble and God-like character is not a thing of favor or chance, but is the natural result of continued effort in right thinking, the effect of long-cherished association with God-like thoughts. An ignoble and bestial character, by the same process, is the result of continued harboring of groveling thoughts.

Man is made or unmade by himself. In the armory of thought he forges the weapons by which he destroys himself. He also fashions the tools with which he builds for himself heavenly mansions of joy and strength and peace. By the right choice and true application of thought, man ascends to the divine perfection. By the abuse and wrong application of thought, he descends below the level of the

A noble and God-like character is not a thing of favor or chance, but is the natural result of continued effort in right thinking, the effect of long-cherished association with God-like thoughts.

beast. Between these two extremes are all the grades of character, and man is their maker and master.

Of all the beautiful truths pertaining to the soul which have been restored and brought to light in this age, none is more gladdening or fruitful of divine promise and confidence than this. That man is the master of thought, the molder of character, and the maker and shaper of condition, environment, and destiny.

As a being of power, intelligence, and love, and the lord of his own thoughts, man holds the key to every situation, and contains within himself that transforming and regenerative agency by which he may make himself what he wills.

Man is always the master, even in his weakest and most abandoned state, but in his weakness and degradation he is the foolish master who misgoverns his household. When he begins to reflect upon his condition, and to search diligently for the law upon which his being is established, then he becomes the wise master, directing his energies with intelligence and fashioning his thoughts to fruitful issues. Such is the conscious master, and man can only thus become by discovering within himself the laws of thought, which discovery is totally a matter of application, self analysis, and experience.

Man can find every truth connected with his being if he will dig deep into the mine of his soul.

Only by much searching and mining are gold and diamonds obtained, and man can find every truth connected with his being if he will dig deep into the mine of his soul, and that he is the maker of his character, the molder of his life, and the builder of his destiny. May he unerringly prove, if he will watch, control, and alter his thoughts, tracing their effects upon himself, upon others, and upon his life and circumstances, linking cause and effect by patient practice and investigation, and utilizing his every experience, even to the most trivial, everyday occurrence, as a means of obtaining that knowledge of himself which is understanding, wisdom, and power. In this direction, as in no other, is the law of absolute that, "He that seeketh findeth; and to him that knocketh it shall be opened." For only by patience, practice, and ceaseless importunity can a man enter the door of the temple of knowledge.

CHAPTER 2

Effect of Thought on Circumstances

Thought and character are one.

Man's mind may be likened to a garden, which may be intelligently cultivated or allowed to run wild. But whether cultivated or neglected, it must, and will, bring forth. If no useful seeds are put into it, then an abundance of useless weed-seeds will fall therein and will continue to produce their kind.

Just as a gardener cultivates his plot, keeping it free from weeds, and growing the flowers and fruits which he requires, so may a man tend the garden of his mind, weeding out all the wrong, useless, and impure thoughts, and cultivating toward perfection the flowers and fruits of right, useful, and pure thoughts. By pursuing this process, a man sooner or later discovers that he is the master-gardener of his soul, the director of his life. He also reveals, within himself, the laws of thought and understands, with ever-increasing accuracy, how the thought-forces and mind elements operate in the shaping of his character, circumstances, and destiny.

Thought and character are one, and as character can only manifest and discover itself through environment and circumstance, the outer conditions of a person's life will always be found to be harmoniously related to his inner state. This does not mean that a man's circumstances at any given time are an indication of his entire character, but that those circumstances are so intimately connected with some vital thought-element within himself that, for the time being, they are indispensable to his development.

Every man is where he is by the law of being. The thoughts which he has built into his character have brought him there, and in the arrangement of his life there is no element of chance, but all is the result of a law which cannot err. This is just as true as those who feel out of harmony with their surroundings as of those who are contented with them.

As a progressive and evolving being, man is where he is that he may learn, that he may grow. And as he learns the

A man sooner or later discovers that he is the master-gardener of his soul, the director of his life.

spiritual lesson which any circumstance contains for him, it passes away and gives place to other circumstances.

Man is buffeted by circumstances so long as he believes himself to be the creature of outside conditions, but when he realizes that he is a creative power, and that he may command the hidden soil and seeds of his being out of which circumstances grow, he then becomes the rightful master of himself.

That circumstances grow out of thought every man knows who has for any length of time practiced self-control and self-purification, for he will have noticed that the alteration in his circumstances has been in exact ratio with his altered mental condition. So true is this that when a man earnestly applies himself to remedy the defects in his character and makes swift and marked progress, he passes rapidly through a succession of vicissitudes.

The soul attracts that which it secretly harbors, that which it loves, and also that which it fears. It reaches the

Man is buffeted by circumstances so long as he believes himself to be the creature of outside conditions, but when he realizes that he is a creative power, he then becomes the rightful master of himself.

height of its cherished aspirations. It falls to the level of its unchastened desires, and circumstances are the means by which the soul receives its own.

Every thought-seed sown or allowed to fall into the mind, and to take root there, produces its own, blossoming sooner or later into act, and bearing its own fruitage of opportunity and circumstance. Good thoughts bear good fruit, bad thoughts bad fruit.

The outer world of circumstance shapes itself to the inner world of thought, and both pleasant and unpleasant external conditions are factors, which make for the ultimate good of the individual. As the reaper of his own harvest, man learns both by suffering and bliss.

Following the inmost desires, aspirations, thoughts, by which he allows himself to be dominated, pursuing the will-o'-the-wisps of impure imaginings or steadfastly walking the highway of strong and high endeavor, a man at last arrives at their fruition and fulfillment in the outer conditions of his life. The laws of growth and adjustment everywhere obtains.

A man does not come to the almshouse or the jail by the tyranny of fate or circumstance, but by the pathway of groveling thoughts and base desires. Nor does a pure-minded man fall suddenly into crime by stress of any mere external force. The criminal thought had long been secretly fostered in the heart, and the hour of opportunity revealed its gathered power. Circumstance does not make the man. It reveals him to himself. No such conditions can exist as descending into vice and its attendant sufferings apart from vicious inclinations, or ascending into virtue and its pure happiness without the continued cultivation of virtuous aspirations. And man, therefore, as the lord and master of thought, is the maker of himself, the shaper and author of environment. Even at birth the soul comes to its own, and through every step of its earthly pilgrimage it attracts those combinations of conditions which reveal itself, which are the reflection of its own purity and impurity, its strength and weakness.

Men do not attract that which they want, but that which they are. Their whims, fancies, and ambitions are thwarted at every step, but their inmost thoughts and desires are fed with their own food, be it foul or clean. The divinity that shapes our ends is in ourselves. It is our very self. Only himself manacles man. Thought and action are the makers of fate. They imprison, being base. And they are also the angels of freedom. They liberate, being noble. Not what he wishes and prays for does a man get, but what he justly earns. His wishes and prayers are only gratified and answered when they harmonize with his thoughts and actions.

Men do not attract that which they want, but that which they are.

In the light of this truth, what then is the meaning of fighting against circumstances? It means that a man is continually revolting against an effect without, while all the time he is nourishing and preserving its cause in his heart. That cause may take the form of a conscious vice or an unconscious weakness, but whatever it is, it stubbornly retards the efforts of its possessor and thus calls aloud for remedy.

Men are anxious to improve their circumstances, but they are unwilling to improve themselves. They therefore remain bound. The man who does not shrink from self-crucifixion can never fail to accomplish the object upon which his heart is set. This is as true of earthly as of heavenly things. Even the man whose sole object is to acquire wealth must be prepared to make great personal sacrifices before he can accomplish his object, and how much more so he who would realize a strong and well-poised life?

Here is a man who is wretchedly poor. He is extremely anxious that his surroundings and home comforts should be improved, yet all the time he shirks his work, and considers he is justified in trying to deceive his employer on the grounds of insufficiency of his wages. Such a man does not understand the simplest rudiments of those principles which are the basis of true prosperity, and is not only totally unfitted to rise out of his wretchedness, but is actually attracting to himself a still deeper wretchedness

Men are anxious to improve their circumstances, but they are unwilling to improve themselves.

by dwelling in and acting out indolent, deceptive, and unmanly thoughts.

Here is a rich man who is the victim of a painful and persistent disease as the result of gluttony. He is willing to give large sums of money to get rid of it, but he will not sacrifice his gluttonous desires. He wants to gratify his taste for rich and unnatural viands and have his health as well. Such a man is totally unfit to have health because he has not yet learned the first principles of a healthy life.

Here is an employer of labor who adopts crooked measures to avoid paying the regulation wage and, in the hope of making larger profits, reduces the wages of his workpeople. Such a man is altogether unfitted for prosperity, and when he finds himself bankrupt, both as regards reputation and riches, he blames circumstances, not knowing that he is the sole author of his condition.

I have introduced these three cases merely as illustrative of the truth that man is the causer, though nearly always is unconsciously, of his circumstances and that, whilst aiming at a good end, he is continually frustrating its accomplishment by encouraging thoughts and desires which cannot possibly harmonize with that end. Such cases could be multiplied and varied almost indefinitely, but this is not necessary, as the reader can, if he so resolves, trace the action of the laws of thought in his own mind and life, and until this is done, mere external facts cannot serve as a ground of reasoning.

Man is the causer, though nearly always is unconsciously, of his circumstances.

Circumstances, however, are so complicated, thought is so deeply rooted, and the conditions of happiness vary so vastly with individuals that a man's entire soul-condition, although it may be known to himself, cannot be judged by another from the external aspect of his life alone. A man may be honest in certain directions, yet suffer privations. A man may be dishonest in certain directions, yet acquire wealth. But the conclusion usually formed that the one man fails because of his particular honesty, and that the other prospers because of his particular dishonesty, is the result of a superficial judgment, which assumes that the dishonest man is almost totally corrupt, and the honest man almost entirely virtuous. In the light of a deeper knowledge and wider experience such judgment is found to be erroneous. The dishonest man may have some admirable virtues which the other does not possess, and the honest man obnoxious vices which are absent in the other. The honest man reaps the good results of his honest thoughts and acts. He also brings upon himself the sufferings which his vices produce. The dishonest man likewise garners his own suffering and happiness.

It is pleasing to human vanity to believe that one suffers because of one's virtue. But not until a man has extirpated every sickly, bitter, and impure thought from his mind, and washed every sinful stain from his soul can he be in a position to know and declare that his sufferings are the result of his good, and not of his bad qualities. And on the way to, yet long before he has reached, that supreme perfection, he will have found, working in his mind and life, the great law which is absolutely just, and which cannot, therefore, give good for evil, evil for good. Possessed of such knowledge, he will then know, looking back upon his past ignorance and blindness, that his life is and always was justly ordered and that all his past experiences, good and bad, were the equitable outworking of his evolving, yet unevolved self.

Good thoughts and actions can never produce bad results. Bad thoughts and actions can never produce good results. This is but saying that nothing can come from corn but corn, nothing from nettles but nettles. Men understand this law in the natural world, and work with it. But few understand it in the mental and moral world, though its operation there is just as simple and undeviating, and they, therefore, do not cooperate with it.

Suffering is always the effect of wrong thought in some direction. It is an indication that the individual is out of harmony with himself, with the law of his being. The sole and supreme use of suffering is to purify, to burn out all that is useless and impure. Suffering ceases for him who is pure. There could be no object in burning gold after the dross had been removed, and a perfectly pure and enlightened being could not suffer.

The circumstances, which a man encounters with blessedness, are the result of his own mental harmony. Blessedness, not material possessions, is the measure of right thought. Wretchedness, not lack of material possessions, is the measure of wrong thought. A man may be cursed and rich. He may be blessed and poor. Blessedness and riches are only joined together when the riches are rightly and wisely used, and the poor man only descends into wretchedness when he regards his lot as a burden unjustly imposed.

Blessedness, not material possessions, is the measure of right thought.

Indigence and indulgence are the two extremes of wretchedness. They are both equally unnatural and the result of mental disorder. A man is not rightly conditioned until he is a happy, healthy, and prosperous being; and happiness, health, and prosperity are the result of a harmonious adjustment of the inner with the outer, of the man with his surroundings.

A man only begins to be a man when he ceases to whine and revile, and commences to search for the hidden justice which regulates his life. And as he adapts his mind to that regulating factor, he ceases to accuse others as the cause of his condition, and builds himself up in strong and noble thoughts, ceases to kick against circumstances, but begins to use them as aids to his more rapid progress, and as a means of discovering the hidden powers and possibilities within himself.

Law, not confusion, is the dominating principle in the universe. Justice, not injustice, is the soul and substance of life. And righteousness, not corruption, is the molding and moving force in the spiritual government of the world. This being so, man has but to right himself to find that the universe is right. And during the process of putting himself right he will find that as he alters his thoughts towards things and other people, things and other people will alter toward him.

A man only begins to be a man when he ceases to whine and revile, and commences to search for the hidden justice which regulates his life.

The proof of this truth is in every person, and it therefore admits of easy investigation by systematic introspection and self-analysis. Let a man radically alter his thoughts, and he will be astonished at the rapid transformation it will effect in the material conditions of his life. Men imagine that thought can be kept secret, but it cannot. It rapidly crystallizes into habit, and habit solidifies into circumstance. Bestial thoughts crystallize into habits of drunkenness and sensuality, which solidify into circumstances of destitution and disease. Impure thoughts of every kind crystallize into enervating and confusing habits, which solidify into distracting and adverse circumstances. Thoughts of fear, doubt, and indecision crystallize into weak, unmanly, and irresolute habits, which solidify into circumstances of failure, indigence, and slavish dependence. Lazy thoughts crystallize into habits of uncleanliness and dishonesty, which solidify into circumstances of foulness and beggary. Hateful and condemnatory thoughts crystallize into habits of accusation and violence, which solidify into circumstances of injury and persecution. Selfish thoughts of all kinds crystallize into habits of self-seeking, which solidify into circumstances more or less distressing.

On the other hand, beautiful thoughts of all kinds crystallize into habits of grace and kindliness, which solidify into genial and sunny circumstances. Pure thoughts crystallize into habits of temperance and self-control, which solidify into circumstances of repose and peace. Thoughts of courage, self-reliance, and decision crystallize into manly habits, which solidify into circumstances of success, plenty, and freedom. Energetic thoughts crystallize into habits of cleanliness and industry, which solidify into circumstances of pleasantness. Gentle and forgiving thoughts crystallize into habits of gentleness, which solidify into protective and preservative circumstances. Loving and unselfish thoughts crystallize into habits of self-forgetfulness for others, which solidify into circumstances of sure and abiding prosperity and true riches.

Beautiful thoughts of all kinds crystallize into habits of grace and kindliness, which solidify into genial and sunny circumstances.

A particular train of thought persisted in, be it good or bad, cannot fail to produce its results on the character and circumstances. A man cannot directly choose his circumstances, but he can choose his thoughts, and so indirectly, yet surely, shape his circumstances.

Nature helps every man to the gratification of the thoughts, which he most encourages, and opportunities are presented which will most speedily bring to the surface both the good and evil thoughts.

Let a man cease from his sinful thoughts, and all the world will soften towards him and be ready to help him. Let him put away his weakly and sickly thoughts, and opportunities will spring up on every hand to aid his strong resolves. Let him encourage good thoughts, and no hard fate shall bind him down to wretchedness and shame. The world is your kaleidoscope, and the varying combinations of colors, which at every succeeding moment it presents to you, are the exquisitely adjusted pictures of your ever-moving thoughts.

A man cannot directly choose his circumstances, but he can choose his thoughts, and so indirectly, yet surely, shape his circumstances.

So you will be what you will to be. Let failure find its false content in that poor word, "environment." But spirit scorns it and is free. It masters time, it conquers space. It cows that boastful trickster chance and bids the tyrant circumstance uncrown and fills a servant's place. The human will, that force unseen, the offspring of a deathless soul, can hew a way to any goal, though walls of granite intervene. Be not impatient in delays, but wait as one who understands. When spirit rises and commands, the gods are ready to obey.

CHAPTER 3

Effect of Thought on Health and the Body

Strong, pure, and happy thoughts build up the body in vigor and grace.

The body is the servant of the mind. It obeys the operations of the mind, whether they be deliberately chosen or automatically expressed. At the bidding of unlawful thoughts the body sinks rapidly into disease and decay. At the command of glad and beautiful thoughts it becomes clothed with youthfulness and beauty.

Disease and health, like circumstances, are rooted in thought. Sickly thoughts will express themselves through a sickly body. Thoughts of fear have been known to kill a man as speedily as a bullet, and they are continually killing thousands of people just as surely, though less rapidly. The people who live in fear of disease are the people who get it. Anxiety quickly demoralizes the whole body, and lays it open to the entrance of disease, while impure thoughts, even if not physically indulged, will soon shatter the nervous system.

Strong, pure, and happy thoughts build up the body in vigor and grace. The body is a delicate and plastic instrument, which responds readily to the thoughts by which it is impressed, and the habits of thought will produce their own effects, good or bad, upon it.

Men will continue to have impure and poisoned blood, so long as they propagate unclean thoughts. Out of a clean heart comes a clean life and a clean body. Out of a defiled mind proceeds a defiled life and a corrupt body. Thought is the fount of action, life, and manifestation. Make the fountain pure, and all will be pure.

Change of diet will not help a man who will not change his thoughts. When a man makes his thoughts pure, he no longer desires impure food.

Clean thoughts make clean habits. The so-called saint who does not wash his body is not a saint. He who has strengthened and purified his thoughts does not need to consider the malevolent microbe.

Out of a clean heart comes a clean life and a clean body. Out of a defiled mind proceeds a defiled life and a corrupt body.

If you would protect your body, guard your mind. If you would renew your body, beautify your mind. Thoughts of malice, envy, disappointment, despondency rob the body of its health and grace. A sour face does not come by chance. It is made by sour thoughts. Wrinkles that mar are drawn by folly, passion, and pride.

I know a woman of 96 who has the bright, innocent face of a girl. I know a man well under middle age whose face is drawn into inharmonious contours. The one is the result of a sweet and sunny disposition, the other is the outcome of passion and discontent.

If you would protect your body, guard your mind. If you would renew your body, beautify your mind.

As you cannot have a sweet and wholesome abode unless you admit the air and sunshine freely into your rooms, so a strong body and a bright, happy, or serene countenance can only result from the free admittance into the mind of thoughts of joy and goodwill and serenity.

On the faces of the aged there are wrinkles made by sympathy, others by strong and pure thought, and others are carved by passion. Who cannot distinguish them? With those who have lived righteously, age is calm, peaceful, and softly mellowed, like the setting sun. I have recently seen a philosopher on his deathbed. He was not old except in years. He died as sweetly and peacefully as he had lived.

There is no physician like a cheerful thought for dissipating the ills of the body. There is no comforter to compare with goodwill for dispersing the shadows of grief and sorrow. To live continually in thoughts of ill will, cynicism, suspicion, and envy is to be confined in a self-made prison hole. But to think well of all, to be cheerful with all, to patiently learn to find the good in all, such unselfish thoughts are the very portals of heaven, and to dwell day by day in thoughts of peace toward every creature will bring abounding peace to their possessor.

CHAPTER 4

Thought and Purpose

Those who have no central purpose in their life fall an easy prey to petty worries, fears, troubles, and self-pityings, all of which lead to failure, unhappiness, and loss.

Until thought is linked with purpose, there is no intelligent accomplishment. With the majority, the bark of thought is allowed to drift upon the ocean of life. Aimlessness is a vice, and such drifting must not continue for him who would steer clear of catastrophe and destruction.

Those who have no central purpose in their life fall an easy prey to petty worries, fears, troubles, and self-pityings, all of which are indications of weakness, which lead, just as surely as deliberately planned sins, though by a different route, to failure, unhappiness, and loss, for weakness cannot persist in a power evolving universe.

A man should conceive of a legitimate purpose in his heart and set out to accomplish it. He should make this purpose the centralizing point of his thoughts. It may take the form of a spiritual ideal, or it may be a worldly object, according to his nature at the time being. But whichever it is, he should steadily focus his thought-forces upon the object, which he has set before him. He should make this purpose his supreme duty and should devote himself to its attainment, not allowing his thoughts to wander away into ephemeral fancies, longings, and imaginings. This is the royal road to self-control and true concentration of thought. Even if he fails again and again to accomplish his purpose, as he necessarily must until weakness is overcome, the strength of character gained will be the measure of his true success, and this will form a new starting point for future power and triumph.

Those who are not prepared for the apprehension of a great purpose should fix the thoughts upon the faultlessness performance of their duty, no matter how insignificant their task may appear. Only in this way can the thoughts be gathered and focused, and resolution and energy be developed, which being done, there is nothing which may not be accomplished.

A man should conceive of a legitimate purpose in his heart and set out to accomplish it.

The weakest soul, knowing its own weakness, and believing this truth that strength can only be developed by effort and practice, will, thus believing, at once begin to exert itself, and, adding effort to effort, patience to patience, and strength to strength, will never cease to develop, and will at last grow divinely strong.

As the physically weak man can make himself strong by careful and patient training, so the man of weak thoughts can make them strong by exercising himself into right thinking.

To put away aimlessness and weakness and to begin to think with purpose is to enter the ranks of those strong ones who only recognize failure as one of the pathways to attainment, who make all conditions serve them, and who think strongly, attempt fearlessly, and accomplish masterfully.

To put away aimlessness and weakness and to begin to think with purpose is to enter the ranks of those strong ones who only recognize failure as one of the pathways to attainment.

Having conceived of his purpose, a man should mentally mark out a straight pathway to its achievement, looking neither to the right nor the left. Doubts and fears should be rigorously excluded. They are disintegrating elements, which break up the straight line of effort, rendering it crooked, ineffectual, useless. Thoughts of doubt and fear never accomplished anything, and never can. They always lead to failure. Purpose, energy, power to do, and all strong thoughts cease when doubt and fear creep in.

The will to do springs from the knowledge that we can do. Doubt and fear are the great enemies of knowledge, and he who encourages them, who does not slay them, thwarts himself at every step.

He who has conquered doubt and fear has conquered failure. His every thought is allied with power, and all difficulties are bravely met and wisely overcome. His purposes are seasonably planted, and they bloom and bring forth fruit, which does not fall prematurely to the ground.

Thoughts allied fearlessly to purpose become creative force. He who knows this is ready to become something higher and stronger than a mere bundle of wavering thoughts and fluctuating sensations. He who does this has become the conscious and intelligent wielder of his mental powers.

CHAPTER 5

The Thought-Factor in Achievement

A strong man cannot help a weaker unless that weaker is willing to be helped.

All that a man achieves and all that he fails to achieve is the direct result of his own thoughts. In a justly ordered universe, where loss of equipoise would mean total destruction, individual responsibility must be absolute. A man's weakness and strength, purity and impurity are his own, and not another man's. They are brought about by himself, and not another. And they can only be altered by himself, never by another. His condition is also his own, and not another man's. His suffering and his happiness are evolved from within. As he thinks, so he is. As he continues to think, so he remains.

A strong man cannot help a weaker unless that weaker is willing to be helped, and even then the weak man must become strong of himself. He must, by his own efforts, develop the strength which he admires in another. None but himself can alter his condition.

It has been usual for men to think and to say, "Many men are slaves because one is an oppressor. Let us hate the oppressor." Now, however, there is amongst an increasing few a tendency to reverse this judgment and to say, "One man is an oppressor because many are slaves. Let us despise the slaves."

The truth is that oppressor and slave are cooperators in ignorance and, while seeming to afflict each other, are in reality afflicting themselves. A perfect knowledge perceives the action of law in the weakness of the oppressed and the misapplied power of the oppressor. A perfect love, seeing the suffering, which both states entail, condemns neither. A perfect compassion embraces both oppressor and oppressed.

He who has conquered weakness and has put away all selfish thoughts belongs neither to oppressor nor oppressed. He is free.

A man can only rise, conquer, and achieve by lifting up his thoughts. He can only remain weak, and abject, and miserable by refusing to lift up his thoughts.

The truth is that oppressor and slave are cooperators in ignorance and, while seeming to afflict each other, are in reality afflicting themselves.

Before a man can achieve anything, even in worldly things, he must lift his thoughts above slavish animal indulgence. He may not, in order to succeed, give up all animality and selfishness, by any means, but a portion of it must, at least, be sacrificed. A man whose first thought is bestial indulgence could neither think clearly nor plan methodically. He could not find and develop his latent resources and would fail in any undertaking. Not having commenced to manfully control his thoughts, he is not in a position to control affairs and to adopt serious responsibilities. He is not fit to act independently and stand alone. But he is limited only by the thoughts, which he chooses.

There can be no progress, no achievement without sacrifice, and a man's worldly success will be in the measure that he sacrifices his confused animal thoughts, and fixes his mind on the development of his plans and the strengthening of his resolution and self-reliance. And the higher he lifts his thoughts, the more manly, upright, and righteous he becomes, the greater will be his success, the more blessed and enduring will be his achievements.

The universe does not favor the greedy, the dishonest, the vicious, although on the mere surface it may sometimes appear to do so. It helps the honest, the magnanimous, the virtuous. All the great teachers of the ages have declared this in varying forms, and to prove and know it a man has but to persist in making himself more and more virtuous by lifting up his thoughts.

There can be no progress, no achievement without sacrifice, and a man's worldly success will be in the measure that he fixes his mind on the development of his plans and the strengthening of his resolution and self-reliance.

Intellectual achievements are the result of thought consecrated to the search for knowledge, or for the beautiful and true in life and nature. Such achievements may be sometimes connected with vanity and ambition, but they are not the outcome of those characteristics. They are the natural outgrowth of long and arduous effort and of pure and unselfish thoughts.

Spiritual achievements are the consummation of holy aspirations. He who lives constantly in the conception of noble and lofty thoughts, who dwells upon all that is pure and unselfish, will, as surely as the sun reaches its zenith and the moon its full, become wise and noble in character and rise into a position of influence and blessedness.

Achievement, of whatever kind, is the crown of effort. By the aid of self-control, resolution, purity, righteousness, and well-directed thought a man ascends. By the aid of animality, indolence, impurity, corruption, and confusion of thought a man descends.

A man may rise to high success in the world, and even to lofty altitudes in the spiritual realm, and again descend into weakness and wretchedness by allowing arrogant, selfish, and corrupt thoughts to take possession of him.

Victories attained by right thought can only be maintained by watchfulness. Many give way when success is assured and rapidly fall back into failure.

He who lives constantly in the conception of noble and lofty thoughts, who dwells upon all that is pure and unselfish, will become wise and noble in character and rise into a position of influence and blessedness.

All achievements, whether in the business, intellectual, or spiritual world, are the result of definitely directed thought, are governed by the same law, and are of the same method. The only difference lies in the object of attainment.

He who would accomplish little must sacrifice little. He who would achieve much must sacrifice much. And he who would attain highly must sacrifice greatly.

CHAPTER 6

Visions and Ideals

He who cherishes a beautiful vision, a lofty ideal in his heart, will one day realize it.

The dreamers are the saviors of the world. As the visible world is sustained by the invisible, so men, through all their trials and sins and sordid vocations, are nourished by the beautiful visions of their solitary dreamers. Humanity cannot forget its dreamers. It cannot let their ideals fade and die. It lives in them. It knows them as the realities which it shall one day see and know.

Composer, sculptor, painter, poet, prophet, sage. These are the makers of the after-world, the architects of heaven. The world is beautiful because they have lived. Without them, laboring humanity would perish.

The dreamers are the saviors of the world.

He who cherishes a beautiful vision, a lofty ideal in his heart, will one day realize it. Columbus cherished a vision of another world, and he discovered it. Copernicus fostered the vision of a multiplicity of worlds and a wider universe, and he revealed it. Buddha beheld the vision of a spiritual world of stainless beauty and perfect peace, and he entered into it.

Cherish your visions. Cherish your ideals. Cherish the music that stirs in your heart, the beauty that forms in your mind, the loveliness that drapes your purest thoughts, for out of them will grow all delightful conditions, all heavenly environment. Of these, if you but remain true to them, your world will at last be built.

The desire is to obtain. To aspire to, to achieve. Shall man's basest desires receive the fullest measure of gratification, and his purest aspirations starve for lack of sustenance? Such is not the law. Such a condition of things can never obtain. Ask and receive.

Dream lofty dreams, and as you dream, so shall you become. Your vision is the promise of what you shall one day be. Your ideal is the prophecy of what you shall at last unveil.

The greatest achievement was at first and for a time a dream. The oak sleeps in the acorn. The bird waits in the egg. And in the highest vision of the soul a waking angel stirs. Dreams are the seedlings of realities.

Your circumstances may be uncongenial, but they shall not long remain so if you but perceive an ideal and strive to reach it. You cannot travel within and stand still without. Here is a youth hard pressed by poverty and labor, confined long hours in an unhealthy workshop, unschooled, and lacking all the arts of refinement. But he dreams of better things. He thinks of intelligence, of refinement, of grace and beauty. He conceives of, mentally builds up, an ideal condition of life. The vision of wider liberty and a larger scope takes possession of him.

Dream lofty dreams, and as you dream, so shall you become.

Unrest urges him to action, and he utilizes all his spare time and means, small though they are, to the development of his latent powers and resources. Very soon so altered has his mind become that the workshop can no longer hold him. It has become so out of harmony with his mentality that it falls out of his life as a garment is cast aside, and with the growth of opportunities, which fit the scope of his expanding powers, he passes out of it forever.

Years later we see this youth as a full-grown man. We find him a master of certain forces of the mind, which he wields with worldwide influence and almost unequaled power. In his hands he holds the cords of gigantic responsibilities. He speaks, and lo, lives are changed. Men and women hang upon his words and remold their characters, and, sun-like, he becomes the fixed and luminous center round which innumerable destinies revolve. He has realized the vision of his youth. He has become one with his ideal.

And you, too, youthful reader, will realize the vision, not the idle wish, of your heart, be it base or beautiful or a mixture of both. For you will always gravitate toward that which you secretly most love. Into your hands will be placed the exact results of your own thoughts. You will receive that which you earn; no more, no less. Whatever your present environment may be, you will fall, remain, or rise with your thoughts, your vision, your ideal. You will become as small as your controlling desire, as great as your dominant aspiration.

You will always gravitate toward that which you secretly most love.

In the beautiful words of Stanton Kirkham Davis, "You may be keeping accounts, and presently you shall walk out of the door that for so long has seemed to you the barrier of your ideals, and shall find yourself before an audience, the pen still behind your ear, the ink stains on your fingers and then and there shall pour out the torrent of your inspiration. You may be driving sheep, and you shall wander to the city open-mouthed, shall wander under the intrepid guidance of the spirit into the studio of the master. And after a time he shall say, 'I have nothing more to teach you.' And now you have become the master, who did so recently dream of great things while driving sheep. You shall lay down the saw and the plane to take upon yourself the regeneration of the world."

You will become as small as your controlling desire, as great as your dominant aspiration.

The thoughtless, the ignorant, and the indolent, seeing only the apparent effects of things and not the things themselves, talk of luck, of fortune, and of chance. Seeing a man grow rich, they say, "How lucky he is." Observing another become intellectual, they exclaim, "How highly favored he is." And noting the saintly character and wide influence of another, they remark, "How chance aids him at every turn." They do not see the trials and failures and struggles which these men have voluntarily encountered in order to gain their experience, have no knowledge of the sacrifices they have made, of the undaunted efforts they have put forth, of the faith they have exercised, that they might overcome the apparently insurmountable, and realize the vision of their heart. They do not know the darkness and the heartaches. They only see the light and joy, and call it "luck." They do not see the long and arduous journey, but only behold the pleasant goal and call it "good fortune." They do not understand the process, but perceive the result and call it chance.

In all human affairs there are efforts, and there are results, and the strength of the effort is the measure of the result. Chance is not. Gifts, powers, material, intellectual, and spiritual possessions are the fruits of effort. They are thoughts completed, objects accomplished, visions realized.

The vision that you glorify in your mind, the ideal that you enthrone in your heart, this you will build your life by, this you will become.

CHAPTER 7

Serenity

The calm man, having learned how to govern himself, knows how to adapt himself to others, and they in turn reverence his spiritual strength and feel that they can learn of him and rely upon him.

Calmness of the mind is one of the beautiful jewels of wisdom. It is the result of long and patient effort in self-control. Its presence is an indication of ripened experience, and of a more than ordinary knowledge of the laws and operations of thought.

A man becomes calm in the measure that he understands himself as a thought evolved being, for such knowledge necessitates the understanding of others as the result of thought. And as he develops a right understanding, and sees more and more clearly the internal relations of things by the action of cause and effect, he ceases to fuss and fume and worry and grieve, and remains poised, steadfast, serene.

The calm man, having learned how to govern himself, knows how to adapt himself to others, and they in turn reverence his spiritual strength and feel that they can learn of him and rely upon him. The more tranquil a man becomes, the greater is his success, his influence, his power for good. Even the ordinary trader will find his business prosperity increase as he develops a greater self-control and equanimity, for people will always prefer to deal with a man whose demeanor is strongly equable.

The strong, calm man is always loved and revered. He is like a shade-giving tree in a thirsty land or a sheltering rock in a storm. Who does not love a tranquil heart, a sweet-tempered, balanced life? It does not matter whether it rains or shines, or what changes come to those possessing these blessings, for they are always sweet, serene, and calm. That exquisite poise of character, which we call serenity, is the last lesson of culture, the fruitage of the soul. It is as precious as wisdom, more to be desired than gold, than even fine gold. How insignificant mere money seeking looks in comparison with a serene life, a life that dwells in the ocean of truth, beneath the waves, beyond the reach of tempests, in the eternal calm.

The more tranquil a man becomes, the greater is his success, his influence, his power for good.

How many people we know who sour their lives, who ruin all that is sweet and beautiful by explosive tempers, who destroy their poise of character, and make bad blood. It is a question whether the great majority of people do not ruin their lives and mar their happiness by lack of self-control. How few people we meet in life who are well-balanced, who have that exquisite poise which is characteristic of the finished character.

Yes, humanity surges with uncontrolled passion. It is tumultuous with ungoverned grief, is blown about by anxiety and doubt. Only the wise man, only he whose thoughts are controlled and purified, makes the winds and the storms of the soul obey him.

Tempest-tossed souls, wherever ye may be, under whatsoever conditions ye may live, know this in the ocean of life, the isles of blessedness are smiling, and the sunny shore of your ideal awaits your coming. Keep your hand firmly upon the helm of thought. In the bark of your soul reclines the commanding master. He does but sleep. Wake him. Self-control is strength. Right thought is mastery. Calmness is power. Say unto your heart, "Peace, be still."

The Mastery of Destiny

James Allen

For man is man and master of his fate.

Preface

The discovery of the law of evolution in the material world has prepared men for a knowledge of the law of cause and effect in the mental world. Thought is not less orderly and progressive than the material forms which embody thought; and not alone cells and atoms, but thoughts and deeds are charged with a cumulative and selective energy. In the realm of thought and deed, the good survives, for it is the "fittest"; the evil ultimately perishes. To know that the "perfect law" of causation is all embracing in mind as in matter is to be relieved from all anxiety concerning the ultimate destiny of individuals and of humanity: "*For man is man and master of his fate.*" And the will in man which is conquering the knowledge of the natural law will conquer the knowledge of the spiritual law. The will which, in ignorance, chooses evil, will, as wisdom evolves and emerges, choose good. In a universe of law, the final mastery of evil by man is assured. His lesser destinies of separation and sorrow, defeat and death, are but disciplinary steps leading to the great destiny of triumphant mastery. He himself is unconsciously building, albeit with lacerated hands and labor-bowed form, the temple of glory which is to afford him an eternal habitation of peace.

In this volume, I have tried to set down some words indicative of this law and this destiny and the manner of its working and its building, and have arranged the subject matter as to make the book a companion volume to the life triumphant. The first six and the last chapters first appeared in the *Bibby's Quarterly* and the *Bibby's Annual* and it is by kind permission of the editor, Mr. Joseph Bibby, that they are now brought together and published in volume form; the other three chapters having been added to make the book consecutive and complete.

James Allen

CHAPTER 1

Deeds, Character, and Destiny

There is, and always has been, a widespread belief in fate, or destiny, that is, in an eternal and inscrutable power which apportions definite ends to both individuals and nations. This belief has arisen from long observation of the facts of life.

People are conscious that there are certain occurrences which they cannot control and are powerless to avert. Birth and death, for instance, are inevitable, and many of the incidents of life appear equally inevitable.

People strain every nerve for the attainment of certain ends, and gradually they become conscious of a power which seems to be not of themselves, which frustrates their puny efforts, and laughs, as it were, at their fruitless striving and struggle.

As people advance in life, they learn to submit, more or less, to this overruling power which they do not understand, perceiving only its effects in themselves and the world around them, and they call it by various names, such as God, providence, fate, destiny, etc.

People of contemplation, such as poets and philosophers, step aside, as it were, to watch the movements of this mysterious power as it seems to elevate its favorites on the one hand and strike down its victims on the other, without reference to merit or demerit.

The greatest poets, especially the dramatic poets, represent this power in their works, as they have observed it in nature. The Greek and Roman dramatists usually depict their heroes as having foreknowledge of their fate and taking means to escape it; but by so doing they blindly involve themselves in a series of consequences which bring about the doom which they are trying to avert. Shakespeare's characters, on the other hand, are represented, as in nature, with no foreknowledge (except in the form of presentiment) of their particular destiny. Thus, according to the poets, whether the person knows their fate or not, they cannot avert it, and every conscious or unconscious act of theirs is a step toward it.

Omar Khayyam's *Moving Finger* is a vivid expression of this idea of Fate:

> *"The Moving Finger writes, and having writ,*
> *Moves on: nor all thy Piety nor Wit*
> *Shall lure it back to cancel half a line,*
> *Nor all thy Tears wash out a Word of it."*

Thus, people in all nations and times have experienced in their lives the action of this invincible power or law, and in our nation today this experience has been crystallized in the terse proverb, "Man proposes, God disposes."

But, contradictory as it may appear, there is an equally widespread belief in man's responsibility as a free agent.

All moral teaching is an affirmation of man's freedom to choose his course and mold his destiny: and man's patient and untiring efforts in achieving his ends are declarations of consciousness of freedom and power.

This dual experience of fate on the one hand, and freedom on the other, has given rise to the interminable controversy between the believers in fatalism and the upholders of free will—a controversy which was recently revived under the term "determinism *versus* freewill."

Between apparently conflicting extremes there is always a "middle way" of balance, justice, or compensation which, while it includes both extremes, cannot be said to be either one or the other, and which brings both into harmony; and this middle way is the point of contact between two extremes.

Truth cannot be a partisan, but, by its nature, is the reconciler of extremes; and so, in the matter which we are considering, there is a "golden mean" which brings fate and free will into close relationship, wherein, indeed, it is seen that these two indisputable facts in human life, for such they are, are but two aspects of one central law, one unifying and all-embracing principle, namely, *the law of causation in its moral aspect.*

Moral causation necessitates both fate and free will, both individual responsibility and individual predestination, for the law of causes must also be the law of effects, and cause and effect must always be equal; the train of causation, both in matter and *mind,* must be eternally balanced, therefore eternally just, eternally perfect. Thus every effect may be said to be a thing *preordained,* but the predetermining power is a cause, and not the fiat of an arbitrary will.

Man finds himself involved in the train of causation. His life is made up of causes and effects. It is both a sowing and a reaping. Each act of his is a cause which must be balanced by its effects. He chooses the cause (this is free will); he cannot choose, alter, or avert the effect (this is fate). Thus free will stands for the power to initiate causes, and destiny is involvement in effects.

It is therefore true that man is predestined to certain ends, but he himself has (though he knows it not) issued the mandate; that good or evil thing from which there is no escape, he has, by his own deeds, brought about.

It may here be urged that man is not responsible for his deeds, that these are the effects of his character, and that he is not responsible for the character, good or bad, which was given him at his birth. If character was "given him" at birth, this would be true, and there would then be no moral law, and no need for moral teaching; but characters are not given ready made, they are evolved; they are, indeed, effects, the products of the moral law itself, that is—the products of deeds. Character results of an accumulation of deeds which have been piled up, so to speak, by the individual during their life.

Man is the doer of his own deeds; as such he is the maker of his own character; and as the doer of his deeds and the maker of his character, he is the molder and shaper of his destiny. He has the power to modify and alter his deeds, and every time he acts he modifies his character, and with the modification of his character for good or evil, he is predetermining for himself new destinies—destinies disastrous or beneficent in accordance with the nature of his deeds. Character is destiny itself; as a fixed combination of deeds, it bears within itself the results of those deeds. These results lie hidden as moral seeds in the dark recesses of the character, awaiting their season of germination, growth, and fruitage.

Those things which befall a person are the reflections of himself; that destiny which pursued him, which he was powerless to escape by effort or avert by prayer, was the relentless ghoul of his own wrong deeds demanding and enforcing restitution; those blessings and curses which come to him unbidden are the reverberating echoes of the sounds which he himself sent forth.

It is this knowledge of the perfect law working through and above all things, of the perfect justice operating in and adjusting all human affairs, that enables the good person to love their enemies and to rise above all hatred, resentment, and complaining; for they know that only their own can come to them, and that, though they be surrounded by persecutors, their enemies are but the blind instruments of a faultless retribution; and so they blame them not, but calmly receive their accounts and patiently pay their moral debts.

But this is not all; they do not merely pay their debts; they take care not to contract any further debts. They watch themselves and make their deeds faultless. While paying off evil accounts, they are laying up good accounts. By putting an end to their own sin, they are bringing evil and suffering to an end.

And now let us consider how the law operates in particular instances in the outworking of destiny through deeds and character. First, we will look at this present life, for the present is the synthesis of the entire past; the net result of all that a man has ever thought and done is contained within him. It is noticeable that sometimes the good person fails and the unscrupulous person prospers—a fact which seems to put all moral maxims as to the good results of righteousness out of account—and because of this, many people deny the operation of any just law in human life, and even declare that it is chiefly the unjust that prosper.

Nevertheless, the moral law exists, and is not altered or subverted by shallow conclusions. It should be remembered that man is a *changing, evolving being*. The good man was not always good; the bad man was not always bad. Even in this life, there was a time, in a large number of instances, when the man who is now just was unjust, when he who is now kind was cruel, when he who is now pure was impure.

Conversely, there was a time in this life, in a number of instances, when he who is now unjust was just, when he who is now cruel was kind, when he who is now impure was pure. Thus, the good man who is overtaken with calamity today is reaping the result of his former evil sowing; later he will reap the happy result of his present good sowing; while the bad man is now reaping the result of his former good sowing; later he will reap the result of his present sowing of bad.

Characteristics are fixed habits of mind, the results of deeds. An act repeated a large number of times becomes unconscious or automatic—that is, it then seems to repeat itself without any effort on the part of the doer, so that it seems to him almost impossible not to do it, and then it has become a mental characteristic.

Here is a poor man out of work. He is honest and is not a shirker. He wants work and cannot get it. He tries hard and continues to fail. Where is the justice in his lot?

There was a time in this man's condition when he had plenty of work. He felt burdened with it; he shirked it, and longed for ease. He thought how delightful it would be to have nothing to do.

He did not appreciate the blessedness of his lot. His desire for ease is now gratified, but the fruit for which he longed, and which he thought would taste so sweet, has turned to ashes in his mouth. The condition which he aimed for, namely, to have nothing to do, he has reached, and there he is compelled to remain till his lesson is thoroughly learned.

And he is surely learning that habitual ease is degrading, that to have nothing to do is a condition of wretchedness, and that work is a noble and blessed thing. His former desires and deeds have brought him where he is; and now his present desire for work, his ceaseless searching and asking for it, will just as surely bring about its own beneficent result. No longer desiring idleness, his present condition will, as an effect, the cause of which is no longer propagated, soon pass away, and he will obtain employment; and if his whole mind is now set on work, and he desires it above all else, then when it comes he will be overwhelmed with it; it will flow in to him from all sides, and he will prosper in his industry.

Then, if he does not understand the law of cause and effect in human life, he will wonder why work comes to him apparently unsought, while others who seek it strenuously fail to obtain it. Nothing comes unbidden; where the shadow is, there also is the substance. That which comes to the individual is the product of his own deeds.

As cheerful industry leads to greater industry and increasing prosperity, and labor shirked or undertaken discontentedly leads to a lesser degree of labor and decreasing prosperity, so with all the varied conditions of life as we see them—they are the destinies wrought by the thoughts and deeds of each particular individual. So also with the vast variety of characters—they are the ripening and ripened growth of the sowing of deeds.

As the individual reaps what he sows, so the nation, being a community of individuals, reaps also what it sows. Nations become great when their leaders are just people; they fall and fade when their just people pass away. Those who are in power set an example, good or bad, for the entire nation.

Great will be the peace and prosperity of a nation when there shall arise within it a line of statesmen and women who, having first established themselves in a lofty integrity of character, shall direct the energies of the nation toward the culture of virtue and development of character, knowing that only through personal industry, integrity, and nobility can national prosperity proceed.

Still, above all, is the great law, calmly and with infallible justice meting out to mortals their fleeting destinies, tear-stained or smiling, the fabric of their hands. Life is a great school for the development of character, and all, through strife and struggle, vice and virtue, success and failure, are slowly but surely learning the lessons of wisdom.

CHAPTER 2

The Science of Self-Control

We live in a scientific age. People of science are numbered by thousands, and they are ceaselessly searching, analyzing, and experimenting with a view to discovery and the increase of knowledge.

The shelves of our libraries, both public and private, are heavy with their load of imposing volumes on scientific subjects, and the wonderful achievements of modern science are always before us—whether in our homes or in our streets, in country or town, on land or sea—there shall we have before us some marvelous device, some recent accomplishment of science, for adding to our comfort, increasing our speed, or saving the labor of our hands.

Yet, with all our vast store of scientific knowledge, and its startling and rapidly increasing results in the world of discovery and invention, there is, in this age, one branch of science which has so far fallen into decay as to have become almost forgotten; a science, nevertheless, which is of greater importance than all the other sciences combined, and without which all science would but sub-serve the ends of selfishness and aid in man's destruction—I refer to the *Science of Self-control.*

Our modern scientists study the elements and forces which are outside themselves with the object of controlling and utilizing them. The ancients studied the elements and forces which were within themselves with a view to controlling and utilizing them, and the ancients produced such mighty masters of knowledge in this direction that to this day they are held in reverence as gods, and the vast religious organizations of the world are based upon their achievements.

Wonderful as are the forces in nature, they are vastly inferior to that combination of intelligent forces which comprise the mind of man, and which dominate and direct the blind mechanical forces of nature. Therefore, it follows that to understand, control, and direct the inner forces of passion, desire, will, and intellect is to be in possession of the destinies of men and nations.

As in ordinary science, there are, in this divine science, degrees of attainment; and a man is great in knowledge, great in himself, and great in his influence on the world in the measure that he is great in self-control.

He who understands and dominates the forces of external nature is the natural scientist; but he who understands and dominates the internal forces of the mind is the divine scientist; and the laws which operate in gaining a knowledge of external appearances operate also in gaining a knowledge of internal varieties.

A man cannot become an accomplished scientist in a few weeks or months, nay, not even in a few years. But only after many years of painstaking investigation can he speak with authority and be ranked among the masters of science. Likewise, a man cannot acquire self-control, and become possessed of the wisdom and peace-giving knowledge which that self-control confers, but by many years of patient labor—a labor which is all the more arduous because it is silent, and both unrecognized and unappreciated by others. He who would pursue this science successfully must learn to stand alone, and to toil unrewarded, as far as any outward emolument is concerned.

The natural scientist pursues, in acquiring his particular kind of knowledge, the following five orderly and sequential steps:

1. *Observation*: that is, he closely and persistently observes the facts of nature.

2. *Experiment*: Having become acquainted, by repeated observations, with certain facts, he experiments with those facts, with a view to the discovery of natural laws. He puts his facts through rigid processes of analysis, and so finds out what is useless and what of value; and he rejects the former and retains the latter.

3. *Classification*: Having accumulated and verified a mass of facts by numberless observations and experiments, he commences to classify those facts, to arrange them in orderly groups with the object of discovering some underlying law, some hidden and unifying principle, which governs, regulates, and binds together these facts.

4. *Deduction*: Thus he passes on to the fourth step of deduction. From the facts and results which are before him, he discovers

certain invariable modes of action, and thus reveals the hidden laws of things.

5. *Knowledge*: Having proven and established certain laws, it may be said of such a man that he *knows*. He is a scientist, a man of knowledge.

But the attainment of scientific knowledge is not the end, great as it is. Men do not attain knowledge for themselves alone, nor to keep it locked secretly in their hearts, like a beautiful jewel in a dark chest. The end of such knowledge is use, service, the increase of the comfort and happiness of the world. Thus, when a man has become a scientist, he gives the world the benefit of his knowledge, and unselfishly bestows upon mankind the results of all his labors.

Thus, beyond knowledge, there is a further step of *Use*: that is, the right and unselfish use of the knowledge acquired; the application of knowledge to invention for the common weal.

It will be noted that the five steps or processes enumerated follow in orderly succession, and that no man can become a scientist who omits any one of them. Without the first step of systematic observation, for instance, he could not even enter the realm of knowledge of nature's secrets.

At first, the searcher for such knowledge has before him a universe of *things*. These things he does not understand; many of them, indeed, seem to be irreconcilably opposed one to the other, and there is apparent confusion; but by patiently and laboriously pursuing these five processes, he discovers the order, nature, and essences of things; perceives the central law or laws which bind them together in harmonious relationship, and so puts an end to confusion and ignorance.

As with the natural scientist, so with the divine scientist. He must pursue, with the same self-sacrificing diligence, five progressive steps in the attainment of self-knowledge, self-control. These five steps are the same as with the natural scientist, but *the process is reversed*. The mind, instead of being centered upon external things, is turned back upon itself, and the investigations are pursued in the realm of mind (of one's own mind) instead of in that of matter.

At first, the searcher for divine knowledge is confronted with that mass of desires, passions, emotions, ideas, and intellections which he calls himself, which is the basis of all his actions, and from which his life proceeds.

This combination of invisible yet powerful forces appears confusedly. Some of them stand, apparently, in direct conflict with each other, without any appearance or hope of reconciliation. His mind in its entirety, too, with his life which proceeds from that mind, does not seem to have any equitable relation to many other minds and lives about him, and altogether there is a condition of pain and confusion from which he would fain escape.

Thus, he begins by keenly realizing his state of ignorance, for no one could acquire either natural or divine knowledge, if he were convinced that without study or labor he already possessed it.

With such perception of one's ignorance, there comes the desire for knowledge, and the novice in self-control enters upon the ascending pathway, in which are the following five steps:

1. INTROSPECTION

This coincides with the *observation* of the natural scientist. The mental eye is turned like a searchlight upon the inner things of the mind, and its subtle and ever varying processes are observed and carefully noted. This stepping aside from selfish gratifications, from the excitements of worldly pleasures and ambitions, in order to observe, with the object of understanding, one's nature, is the beginning of self-control. Hitherto, the man has been blindly and impotently borne along by the impulses of his nature, the mere creature of things and circumstances, but now he puts a check upon his impulses and, instead of being controlled, begins to control.

2. SELF-ANALYSIS

Having observed the tendencies of the mind, they are then closely examined, and are put through a rigid process of analysis. The evil tendencies (those that produce painful effects) are separated from the good tendencies (those that produce peaceful effects); and the various tendencies, with the particular actions they produce, and the definite results which invariably spring from these actions, are gradually grasped by the understanding, which is at last enabled to follow them in their swift and subtle interplay and profound ramifications. It is a process of *testing and proving*, and, for the searcher, a period of being tested and proved.

3. ADJUSTMENT

By this time, the practical student of things divine has clearly before him every tendency and aspect of his nature, down to the profoundest promptings of his mind, and the most subtle motives of his heart. There is not a spot or corner left, which he has not explored and illuminated with the light of self-examination.

He is familiar with every weak and selfish point, every strong and virtuous quality. It is considered the height of wisdom to be able to see ourselves as others see us, but the practitioner of self-control goes far beyond this: he not only sees himself as others see him, *he sees himself as he is*. Thus, standing face to face with himself, not striving to hide away from any secret fault; no longer defending himself with pleasant flatteries; neither underrating nor overrating himself or his powers, and no more cursed with self-praise or self-pity, he sees the full magnitude of the task which lies before him, sees dearly ahead the heights of self-control, and knows what work he has to do to reach them.

He is no longer in a state of confusion, but has gained a glimpse of the laws which operate in the world of thought, and he now begins to *adjust* his mind in accordance with those laws. This is a process of *weeding, sifting, cleansing.* As the farmer weeds, cleans, and prepares the ground for his crops, so the student removes the weeds of evil from his mind, cleanses and purifies it preparatory to sowing the seeds of righteous actions which shall produce the harvest of a well ordered life.

4. RIGHTEOUSNESS

Having adjusted his thoughts and deeds to those minor laws which operate in mental activities in the production of pain and pleasure, unrest and peace, sorrow and bliss, he now perceives that there is involved in those laws one great central law which, like the law of gravitation in the natural world, is supreme in the world of mind—a law to which all thoughts and deeds are subservient, and by which they are regulated and kept in their proper sphere.

This is the law of *justice* or *righteousness,* which is universal and supreme. To this law he now conforms. Instead of thinking and acting blindly, as the nature is stimulated and appealed to by outward things, he subordinates his thoughts and deeds to this central principle. He no longer acts from self, *but does what is right*—what is universally and eternally right. He is no longer the abject slave of his nature and circumstances, he is the master of his nature and circumstances.

He is no longer carried hither and thither on the forces of his mind; he controls and guides those forces to the accomplishment of his purposes. Thus, having his nature in control and subjection, not thinking thoughts nor doing deeds which oppose the righteous law, and which, therefore, that law annuls with suffering and defeat, he rises above the dominion of sin and sorrow, ignorance and doubt, and is strong, calm, and peaceful.

5. PURE KNOWLEDGE

By thinking right and acting right, he proves, by experience, the existence of the divine law on which the mind is framed, and which is the guiding and unifying principle in all human affairs and events, whether individual or national. Thus, by perfecting himself in self-control, he acquires divine knowledge; he reaches the point where it may be said of him, as of the natural scientist, that he *knows*.

He has mastered the science of self-control, and has brought knowledge out of ignorance, order out of confusion. He has acquired that knowledge of self which includes knowledge of all men, that knowledge of one's own life which embraces knowledge of all life. As all minds are the same in essence (differing only in degree), are framed upon the same law and the same thoughts and acts, by whatsoever individual they are wrought, they will always produce the same results.

But this divine and peace bestowing knowledge, as in the case of the natural scientist, is not gained for one's self alone. If this were so, the aim of evolution would be frustrated, and it is not in the nature of things to fall short of ripening and accomplishment; and, indeed, he who thought to gain this knowledge solely for his own happiness would most surely fail.

So, beyond the *fifth* step of *pure knowledge,* there is a still further one of *wisdom,* which is the right application of the knowledge acquired—the pouring out upon the world, unselfishly and without stint, the result of one's labors, thus accelerating progress and uplifting humanity.

It may be said of people who have not gone back into their own nature to control and purify it that they cannot clearly distinguish between good and evil, right and wrong. They reach after those things which they think will give them pleasure, and try to avoid those things which they believe will cause them pain.

The source of their actions is self, and they only discover right painfully and in a fragmentary way, by periodically passing through severe sufferings and lashings of conscience. But the one who practices self-control, passing through the five processes, which are five stages of growth, gains that knowledge which enables them to act from the moral law which sustains the universe. They know good and evil, right and wrong, and, thus knowing them, live in accordance with good and right. They no longer need to consider what is pleasant or what is unpleasant, but do what is right; their nature is in harmony with their conscience, and there is no remorse; their mind is in unison with the great law, and there is no more suffering and sin; for them, evil is ended and good is all in all.

CHAPTER 3

Cause and Effect in Human Conduct

It is an axiom with the scientists that every effect is related to a cause. Apply this to the realm of human conduct, and there is revealed the principle of *justice*.

Every scientist knows (and now all people believe) that perfect harmony prevails throughout every portion of the physical universe, from the speck of dust to the greatest sun. Everywhere there is exquisite adjustment. In the sidereal universe, with its millions of suns rolling majestically through space and carrying with them their respective systems of revolving planets, its vast nebulae, its seas of meteors, and its vast army of comets traveling through illimitable space with inconceivable velocity, perfect order prevails. Again, in the natural world, with its multitudinous aspects of life, and its infinite variety of forms, there are the clearly defined limits of specific laws, through the operation of which all confusion is avoided, and unity and harmony eternally obtain.

If this universal harmony could be arbitrarily broken, even in one small particular, the universe would cease to be; there could be no cosmos, but only universal chaos. Nor can it be possible in such a universe of law that there should exist any personal power which is above, outside, and superior to such law in the sense that it can defy it or set it aside; for whatsoever beings exist, whether they be human or gods, they exist by virtue of such law; and the highest, best, and wisest among all beings would manifest their greater wisdom by their more complete obedience to that law which is wiser than wisdom and than which nothing more perfect could be devised.

All things, whether visible or invisible, are subservient to, and fall within the scope of, this infinite and eternal law of *causation*. As all things seen obey it, so all things unseen—the thoughts and deeds of men, whether secret or open—cannot escape it.

> *"Do right, it recompenseth; do one wrong,*
> *the equal retribution must be made."*

Perfect justice upholds the universe; perfect justice regulates human life and conduct. All the varying conditions of life, as they obtain in the world today, are the result of this law reacting on human conduct. Man can (and does) choose what causes he shall set in operation, but he cannot change the nature of effects; he can decide what thoughts he shall think, and what deeds he shall do, but he has no power over the *results* of those thoughts and deeds. These are regulated by the overruling law.

Man has all power to act, but his power ends with the act committed. The result of the act cannot be altered, annulled, or escaped; it is irrevocable. Evil thoughts and deeds produce conditions of suffering; good thoughts and deeds determine conditions of blessedness. Thus man's power is limited to and his blessedness or misery is determined by *his own conduct*. To know this truth renders life simple, *plain*, and unmistakable; all the crooked paths are straightened out, the heights of wisdom are revealed, and the open door to salvation from evil and suffering is perceived and entered.

Life may be likened to a sum in arithmetic. It is bewilderingly difficult and complex to the pupil who has not yet grasped the key to its correct solution, but once this is perceived and laid hold of, it becomes as astonishingly simple as it was formerly profoundly perplexing. Some idea of this relative simplicity and complexity of life may be grasped by fully recognizing and realizing the fact that, while there are scores, and perhaps hundreds, of ways in which a sum may be done wrong, *there is only one way by which it can be done right,* and that when that right way is found the pupil *knows it to be the right;* his perplexity vanishes, and he knows that he has mastered the problem.

It is true that the pupil, while doing his sum incorrectly, may (and frequently does) *think* he has done it correctly, but he is not sure; his perplexity is still there, and if he is an earnest and apt pupil, he will recognize his own error when it is pointed out by the teacher. So in life, men may think they are living rightly while they are continuing, through ignorance, to live wrongly; but the presence of doubt, perplexity, and unhappiness are sure indications that the right way has not yet been found.

There are foolish and careless pupils who would like to pass a sum as correct before they have acquired a true knowledge of figures, but the eye and skill of the teacher quickly detect and expose the fallacy. So in life there can be no falsifying of results; the eye of the great law reveals and exposes. Twice five will make ten to all eternity, and no amount of ignorance, stupidity, or delusion can bring the result up to eleven.

If one looks superficially at a piece of cloth, he sees it as a piece of cloth, but if he goes further and inquires into its manufacture, and examines it closely and attentively, he sees that it is composed of a combination of individual threads, and that, while all the threads are interdependent, each thread pursues its own way throughout, never becoming confused with its sister thread. It is this entire absence of confusion between the particular threads which constitutes the finished work a *piece of cloth*; any inharmonious commingling of the thread would result in a bundle of *waste* or a useless *rag*.

Life is like a piece of cloth, and the threads of which it is composed are individual lives. The threads, while being interdependent, are not confounded one with the other. Each follows its own course. Each individual suffers and enjoys the consequences of his own deeds, and not of the deeds of another. The course of each is simple and definite; the whole forming a complicated, yet harmonious, combination of sequences. There are action and reaction, deed and consequence, cause and effect, and the counterbalancing reaction, consequence, and effect is always in exact ratio with the initiatory impulse.

A durable and satisfactory piece of cloth cannot be made from shoddy material, and the threads of selfish thoughts and bad deeds will not produce a useful and beautiful life—a life that will wear well, and bear close inspection. Each man makes or mars his own life; it is not made or marred by his neighbor, or by anything external to himself. Each thought he thinks, each deed he does, is another thread—shoddy or genuine—woven into the garment of his life; and as he makes the garment so must he wear it. He is not responsible for his neighbor's deeds; he is not the custodian of his neighbor's actions; he is responsible only for his own deeds; he is the custodian of his own actions.

The "problem of evil" subsists in a man's own evil deeds, and it is solved when those deeds are purified. Says Rousseau:

> *"Man, seek no longer the origin of*
> *evil; thou thyself art its origin."*

Effect can never be divorced from cause; it can never be of a different nature from cause. Emerson says:

> *"Justice is not postponed; a perfect equity*
> *adjusts the balance in all parts of life."*

And there is a profound sense in which cause and effect are simultaneous, and form one perfect whole. Thus, upon the instant that a person thinks, say, a cruel thought, or does a cruel deed, that same instant they have *injured their own mind*; they are not the same *person* they were the previous instant. They are a little viler and a little more unhappy; and a number of such successive thoughts and deeds would produce a cruel and wretched person. The same thing applies to the contrary—the thinking of a kind thought, or doing a kind deed. An immediate nobility and happiness attend it; the person is better than they were before, and a number of such deeds would produce a great and blissful soul.

Thus individual human conduct determines, by the faultless law of cause and effect, individual merit or demerit, individual greatness or meanness, individual happiness or wretchedness. What a person thinks, that he does; what he does, that he is. If he is perplexed, unhappy, restless, or wretched, let him look to himself, for there and nowhere else is the source of all his trouble.

CHAPTER 4

Training of the Will

Without strength of mind, nothing worthy of accomplishment can be done, and the cultivation of that steadfastness and stability of character which is commonly called "willpower" is one of the foremost duties of man, for its possession is essentially necessary both to his temporal and eternal wellbeing. Fixedness of purpose is at the root of all successful efforts, whether in things worldly or spiritual, and without it man cannot be otherwise than wretched, and dependent upon others for that support which should be found within himself.

The mystery, which has been thrown around the subject of cultivation of the will by those who advertise to sell "occult advice" on the matter for so many dollars, should be avoided and dispelled, for nothing could be further removed from secrecy and mystery than the practical methods by which alone strength of will can be developed.

The true path of will cultivation is only to be found in the common everyday life of the individual, and so obvious and simple is it that the majority, looking for something complicated and mysterious, pass it by unnoticed.

A little logical thought will soon convince a person that they cannot be both weak and strong at the same time, that they cannot develop a stronger will while remaining a slave to weak indulgences, and that, therefore, the direct and only way to that greater strength is to assail and conquer their weaknesses. All the means for the cultivation of the will are already at hand in the mind and life of the individual; they reside in the weak side of their character, by attacking and vanquishing which the necessary strength of will be developed. A person who has succeeded in grasping this simple, preliminary truth will perceive that the whole science of will cultivation is embodied in the following seven rules:

1. Break off bad habits.

2. Form good habits.

3. Give scrupulous attention to the duty of the present moment.

4. Do vigorously, and at once, whatever has to be done.

5. Live by rule.

6. Control the tongue.

7. Control the mind.

Anyone who earnestly meditates upon and diligently practices the above rules will not fail to develop that purity of purpose and power of will which will enable them to successfully cope with every difficulty and pass triumphantly through every emergency.

It will be seen that the first step is the breaking away from bad habits. This is no easy task. It demands the putting forth of great efforts, or a succession of efforts, and it is by such efforts that the will can alone be invigorated and fortified. If one refuses to take the first step, they cannot increase in willpower, for by submitting to a bad habit, because of the immediate pleasure which it affords, one forfeits the right to rule over themselves, and they are so far a weak slave. Those who thus avoid self-discipline and look about for some "occult secrets" for gaining willpower, at the expenditure of little or no effort on their part, are deluding themselves and are weakening the willpower which they already possesses.

The increased strength of will which is gained by success in overcoming bad habits enables one to initiate good habits; for, while the conquering of a bad habit requires merely strength of purpose, the forming of a new one necessitates the *intelligent direction of purpose*. To do this, a person must be mentally active and energetic and must keep a constant watch upon themselves. As a person succeeds in perfecting themselves in the second rule, it will not be very difficult for them to observe the third—that of giving scrupulous attention to the duty of the present moment.

Thoroughness is a step in the development of the will which cannot be passed over. Slipshod work is an indication of weakness. Perfection should be aimed at, even in the smallest task. By not dividing the mind, but giving the whole attention to each separate task as it presents itself, singleness of purpose and intense concentration of mind are gradually gained—two mental powers which give weight and worth of character and bring repose and joy to their possessor.

The fourth rule—that of doing vigorously and at once whatever has to be done—is equally important. Idleness and a strong will cannot go together, and procrastination is a total barrier to the acquisition of purposeful action. *Nothing* should be "put off" until another time, not even for a few minutes. That which ought to be done now should be done now. This seems a little thing, but it is of far-reaching importance. It leads to strength, success, and peace.

The person who is to manifest a cultivated will must also live by certain fixed rules. They must not blindly gratify their passions and impulses, but must school them to obedience. They should live according to principle and not according to passion.

They should decide what they will eat and drink and wear, and what they will not eat and drink and wear; how many meals per day they will have, and at what times they will have them; at what time they will go to bed, and at what time get up. They should make rules for the right government of their conduct in every department of their life and should religiously adhere to them. To live loosely and indiscriminately, eating and drinking and sensually indulging at the beck and call of appetite and inclination, is to be a mere animal and not a human with will and reason.

The beast in man must be scourged and disciplined and brought into subjection, and this can only be done by training the mind and life on certain fixed rules of right conduct. The saint attains to holiness by not violating their vows, and the person who lives according to good and fixed rules is strong to accomplish their purpose.

The sixth rule, that of controlling the tongue, must be practiced until one has perfect command of their speech, so that they utter nothing in peevishness, anger, irritability, or with evil intent. The person of strong will does not allow their tongue to run thoughtlessly and without check.

All these six rules, if faithfully practiced, will lead up to the seventh, which is the most important of them all—namely, rightly controlling the mind. Self-control is the most essential thing in life, yet least understood; but he who patiently practices the rules herein laid down, bringing them into requisition in all his ways and undertakings, will learn, by his own experience and efforts, how to control and train his mind and to earn thereby the supreme crown of humanity—the crown of a perfectly poised will.

CHAPTER 5

Thoroughness

Thoroughness consists in doing little things as though they were the greatest things in the world. That the little things of life are of primary importance is a truth not generally understood, and the thought that little things can be neglected, thrown aside, or slurred over is at the root of that lack of thoroughness which is so common, and which results in imperfect work and unhappy lives.

When one understands that the great things of the world and of life consist of a combination of small things, and that without this aggregation of small things the great things would be nonexistent, then they begin to pay careful attention to those things which they formerly regarded as insignificant. They thus acquire the quality of thoroughness and become a person of usefulness and influence; for the possession or non-possession of this one quality may mean all the difference between a life of peace and power and one of misery and weakness.

Every employer of labor knows how comparatively rare this quality is—how difficult it is to find men and women who will put thought and energy into their work and do it completely and satisfactorily. Bad workmanship abounds. Skill and excellence are acquired by few. Thoughtlessness, carelessness, and laziness are such common vices that it should cease to appear strange that, in spite of "social reform," the ranks of the unemployed should continue to swell, for those who scamp their work today will, another day, in the hour of deep necessity, look and ask for work in vain.

The law of the survival of the fittest is not based on cruelty, it is based on justice: it is one aspect of that divine equity which everywhere prevails. Vice is "beaten with many stripes"; if it were not so, how could virtue be developed? The thoughtless and lazy cannot take precedence of, or stand equally with, the thoughtful and industrious. A friend of mine tells me that his father gave all his children the following piece of advice:

> *"Whatever your future work may be, put your whole mind upon it and do it thoroughly; you*

need then have no fear as to your welfare, for there are so many who are careless and negligent that the services of the thorough man are always in demand."

I know those who have, for years, tried almost in vain to secure competent workmanship in spheres which do not require exceptional skill, but which call chiefly for forethought, energy, and conscientious care. They have discharged one after another for negligence, laziness, incompetence, and persistent breaches of duty—not to mention other vices which have no bearing on this subject—yet the vast army of the unemployed continues to cry out against the laws, against society, and against Heaven.

The cause of this common lack of thoroughness is not far to seek; it lies in that thirst for pleasure which not only creates a distaste for steady labor, but renders one incapable of doing the best work, and of properly fulfilling one's duty. A short time ago, a case came under my observation (one of many such) of a poor woman who was given, at her earnest appeal, a responsible and lucrative position. She had been at her post only a few days when she began to talk of the "pleasure trips" she was going to have now she had come to that place. She was discharged at the end of a month for negligence and incompetence.

As two objects cannot occupy the same space at the same time, so the mind that is occupied with pleasure cannot also be concentrated upon the perfect performance of duty.

Pleasure has its own place and time, but its consideration should not be allowed to enter the mind during those hours which should be devoted to duty. Those who, while engaged in their worldly task, are continually dwelling upon anticipated pleasures, cannot do otherwise than bungle through their work, or even neglect it when their pleasure seems to be at stake.

Thoroughness is completeness, perfection; it means doing a thing so well that there is nothing left to be desired; it means doing one's work, if not better than anyone else can do it, at least not worse than the best that others do. It means the exercise of much thought, the putting forth of great energy, the persistent application of the mind to its task, the cultivation of patience, perseverance, and a high sense of duty. An ancient teacher said, "If anything has to be done, let a man do it, let him attack it vigorously"; and another teacher said, "Whatsoever thy hand findeth to do, do it with thy might."

He who lacks thoroughness in his worldly duties will also lack the same quality in spiritual things. He will not improve his character, will be weak and half-hearted in his religion, and will not accomplish any good and useful end. The person who keeps one eye on worldly pleasure and the other on religion, and who thinks he can have the advantage of both conditions, will not be thorough either in his pleasure seeking or his religion, but will make a sorry business of both. It is better to be a whole-souled worldling than a half-hearted religionist; better to give the entire mind to a lower thing than half of it to a higher.

It is preferable to be thorough, even if it be in a bad or selfish direction, rather than inefficient and squeamish in good directions, for thoroughness leads more rapidly to the development of character and the acquisition of wisdom; it accelerates progress and unfoldment; and while it leads the bad to something better, it spurs the good to higher and ever higher heights of usefulness and power.

CHAPTER 6

Mind-Building and Life-Building

Everything, both in nature and the works of man, is produced by a process of building. The rock is built up of atoms; the plant, the animal, and man are built up of cells; a house is built of bricks, and a book is built of letters. A world is composed of a large number of forms, and a city of a large number of houses. The arts, sciences, and institutions of a nation are built up by the efforts of individuals. The history of a nation is the building of its deeds.

The process of building necessitates the alternate process of breaking down. Old forms that have served their purpose are broken up, and the material of which they are composed enters into new combinations. There is reciprocal integration and disintegration. In all compounded bodies, old cells are ceaselessly being broken up, and new cells are formed to take their place.

The works of man also require to be continually renewed until they have become old and useless, when they are torn down in order that some better purpose may be served. These two processes of breaking down and building up in nature are called *death* and *life*; in the artificial works of man they are called *destruction* and *restoration*.

This dual process, which obtains universally in things visible, also obtains universally in things invisible. As a body is built of cells and a house of bricks, so a person's mind is built of thoughts. The various characters of individuals are none other than compounds of thoughts of varying combinations. Herein we see the deep truth of the saying, "As a man thinketh in his heart, so is he." Individual characteristics are fixed *processes of thought*; that is, they are fixed in the sense that they have become such an integral part of the character that they can be only altered or removed by a protracted effort of the will and by much self-discipline. Character is built in the same way as a tree or a house is built—namely, by the ceaseless addition of new material, and that material is *thought*. By the aid of millions of bricks a city is built; by the aid of millions of thoughts a mind, a character, is built.

Everyone is a mind builder, whether they recognize it or not. Everyone must perforce think, and every thought is another brick laid down in the edifice of mind. Such "brick laying" is done loosely and carelessly by a vast number of people, the result being unstable and tottering characters that are ready to go down under the first little gust of trouble or temptation.

Some, also, put into the building of their minds large numbers of impure thoughts; these are so many rotten bricks that crumble away as fast as they are put in, leaving always an unfinished and unsightly building, and one which can afford no comfort and no shelter for its possessor.

Debilitating thoughts about one's health, enervating thoughts concerning unlawful pleasures, weakening thoughts of failure, and sickly thoughts of self-pity and self-praise are useless bricks with which no substantial mind temple can be raised.

Pure thoughts, wisely chosen and well placed, are so many durable bricks which will never crumble away, and from which a finished and beautiful building, and one which affords comfort and shelter for its possessor, can be rapidly erected.

Bracing thoughts of strength, of confidence, of duty and inspiring thoughts of a large, free, unfettered, and unselfish life are useful bricks with which a substantial mind temple can be raised; and the building of such a temple necessitates that old and useless habits of thought be broken down and destroyed.

> *"Build thee more stately mansions, O*
> *my soul! As the swift seasons roll."*

Each person is the builder of himself. If they are the occupant of a jerry-built hovel of a mind that lets in the rains of many troubles, and through which blow the keen winds of oft-recurring disappointments, let them get to work to build a more noble mansion which will afford them better protection against those mental elements. Trying to weakly shift the responsibility for their jerry-building on to the devil, or their forefathers, or anything or anybody but themselves will neither add to their comfort nor help them to build a better habitation.

When they wake up to a sense of their responsibility and an approximate estimate of their power, then they will commence to build like a true worker, and will produce a symmetrical and finished character that will endure and be cherished by posterity, and which, while affording a never failing protection for themselves, will continue to give shelter to many a struggling one when they have passed away.

The whole visible universe is framed on a few mathematical principles. All the wonderful works of man in the material world have been brought about by the rigid observance of a few underlying principles; and all that there is to the making of a successful, happy, and beautiful life is the knowledge and application of a few simple, root principles.

If a person is to erect a building that is to resist the fiercest storms, they must build it on a simple, mathematical principle, or law, such as the square or the circle; if they ignore this, their edifice will topple down even before it is finished.

Likewise, if a person is to build up a successful, strong, and exemplary life—a life that will stoutly resist the fiercest storms of adversity and temptation—it must be framed on a few simple, undeviating moral principles.

Four of these principles are *justice, rectitude, sincerity,* and *kindness*. These four ethical truths are to the making of a life what the four lines of a square are to the building of a house. If a person ignores them and thinks to obtain success and happiness and peace by injustice, trickery, and selfishness, they are in the position of a builder who imagines he can build a strong and durable habitation while ignoring the relative arrangement of mathematical lines, and they will, in the end, obtain only disappointment and failure.

They may, for a time, make money, which will delude them into believing that injustice and dishonesty pay well; but in reality their life is so weak and unstable that it is ready at any moment to fall. When a critical period comes, as come it must, their affairs, their reputation, and their riches crumble to ruins, and they are buried in their own desolation.

It is totally impossible for a person to achieve a truly successful and happy life who ignores the four moral principles enumerated, whilst the person who scrupulously observes them in all their dealings can no more fail of success and blessedness than the earth can fail of the light and warmth of the sun so long as it keeps to its lawful orbit; for they are working in harmony with the fundamental laws of the universe; they are building their life on a basis which cannot be altered or overthrown, and, therefore, all that they do will be so strong and durable, and all the parts of their life will be so coherent, harmonious, and firmly knit that it cannot possibly be brought to ruin.

In all the universal forms which are built up by the great invisible and unerring power, it will be found that the observance of mathematical law is carried out with unfailing exactitude down to the most minute detail. The microscope reveals the fact that the infinitely small is as perfect as the infinitely great.

A snowflake is as perfect as a star. Likewise, in the erection of a building, the strictest attention must be paid to every detail.

A foundation must first be laid, and, although it is to be buried and hidden, it must receive the greatest care and be made stronger than any other part of the building; then stone upon stone, brick upon brick is carefully laid with the aid of the plumb line, until at last the building stands complete in its durability, strength, and beauty.

Even so it is with the life of an individual. One who would have a life secure and blessed, a life freed from the miseries and failures to which so many fall victim, must carry the practice of the moral principles into every detail of their life, into every momentary duty and trivial transaction. In every little thing they need be thorough and honest, neglecting nothing.

To neglect or misapply any little detail—be they commercial people, agriculturists, professional people, or artisans—is the same as neglecting a stone or a brick in a building, and it will be a source of weakness and trouble.

The majority of those who fail and come to grief do so through neglecting the apparently *insignificant* details.

It is a common error to suppose that little things can be passed by, and that the greater things are more important, and should receive all attention; but a cursory glance at the universe, as well as a little serious reflection on life, will teach the lesson that nothing great can exist which is not made up of small details, and in the composition of which every detail is perfect.

One who adopts the four ethical principles as the law and base of their life, who raises the edifice of character upon them, who in his thoughts and words and actions does not wander from them, whose every duty and every passing transaction is performed in strict accordance with their exactions, such a person, laying down the hidden foundation of integrity of heart securely and strongly, cannot fail to raise up a structure which shall bring them honor; and they are building a temple in which they can repose in peace and blessedness—even the strong and beautiful temple of their life.

CHAPTER 7

Cultivation of Concentration

Concentration, or the bringing of the mind to a center and keeping it there, is vitally necessary to the accomplishment of any task. It is the father of *thoroughness* and the mother of *excellence*. As a faculty, it is not an end in itself, but is an aid to all faculties, all work. Not a purpose in itself, it is yet a power which serves all purposes. Like steam in mechanics, it is a dynamic force in the machinery of the mind and the functions of life.

The faculty is a common possession, though in its perfection it is rare—just as *will* and *reason* are common possessions, though a perfectly poised will and a comprehensive reason are rare possessions—and the mystery which some modern mystical writers have thrown around it is entirely superfluous.

Every successful individual, in whatever direction their success may lie, practices concentration, though they may know nothing about it as a subject of study; every time one becomes absorbed in a book or task, or is rapt in devotion or assiduous in duty, concentration, in a greater or lesser degree, is brought into play.

Many books purporting to give instructions on concentration make its practice *and* acquisition an end in itself. Than this, there is no surer nor swifter way to its destruction. The fixing of the eyes upon the tip of the nose, upon a doorknob, a picture, a mystical symbol, or the portrait of a saint; or the centering of the mind upon the navel, the pineal gland, or some imaginary point in space (I have seen all these methods seriously advised in works on this subject) with the object of acquiring concentration, is like trying to nourish the body by merely moving the jaw as in the act of eating, without taking food. Such methods prevent the end at which they aim.

They lead toward dispersion and not concentration; toward weakness and imbecility rather than toward power and intelligence. I have met those who have squandered, by these practices, what measure of concentration they at first possessed, and have become the prey of a weak and wandering mind.

Concentration is an aid to the doing of something; it is not the doing of something in itself. A ladder has no value in and of itself, but only in so far as it enables us to reach something which we could not otherwise reach. In like manner, concentration is that which enables the mind to accomplish with ease that which it would otherwise be impossible to accomplish; but of itself is a dead thing and not a living accomplishment.

Concentration is so interwoven with the uses of life that it cannot be separated from duty; and one who tries to acquire it apart from their task, their duty, will not only fail but diminish, and not increase, their mental control and executive capacity, and so render themselves less and less fit to succeed in their undertakings.

In the task of the hour is all the means for the cultivation of concentration—whether the task be the acquiring of divine knowledge or the sweeping of a floor—without resorting to methods which have no practical bearing on life; for what is concentration but the bringing of a well controlled mind to the doing of that which has to be done?

One who does their work in an aimless, a hurried, or thoughtless manner, and resorts to their artificial "concentration methods"—to their doorknob, their picture, or nasal extremity—in order to gain that which they imagine to be some kind of mystical power—but which is a very ordinary and practical quality—though they may drift toward insanity (and I knew one man who became insane by these practices), they will not increase in steadiness of mind.

The great enemy of concentration—and therefore of all skill and power—is a wavering, wandering, undisciplined value in and of itself, but only in so far as it enables us to *reach* something which we could not otherwise reach. In like manner, concentration is that which enables the mind to accomplish with ease that which it would be otherwise impossible to accomplish; but of itself it is a dead thing, and not a living accomplishment.

Concentration is so interwoven with the uses of life that it cannot be separated from duty; and one who tries to acquire it *apart from their task, their duty,* will not only fail, but will diminish, and not increase, their mental control and executive capacity, and so render themselves less and less fit to succeed in their undertakings.

A scattered and undisciplined army would be useless. To make it effective in action and swift in victory it must be solidly concentrated and masterfully directed. Scattered and diffused thoughts are weak and worthless. Thoughts marshaled, commanded, and directed upon a given point are invincible; confusion, doubt, and difficulty give way before their masterly approach. Concentrated thought enters largely into all successes and informs all victories.

There is no more secret about its acquirement than about any other acquisition, for it is governed by the underlying principle of all development, namely, *practice*. To be able to do a thing, you must begin to *do it*, and keep on doing it until the thing is mastered. This principle prevails universally—in all arts, sciences, trades; in all learning, conduct, religion. To be able to paint, one must paint; to know how to use a tool skillfully, one must use the tool; to become learned, one must learn; to become wise, one must do wise things; and to successfully concentrate the mind, one must concentrate it. But the doing is not all—*it must be done with energy and intelligence*.

The beginning of concentration, then, is to go to your daily task and put your mind on it, bringing all your intelligence and mental energy to a focus upon that which has to be done; and every time the thoughts are found wandering aimlessly away, they should be brought promptly back to the thing in hand.

Thus the "center" upon which you are to bring your mind to a point is not your pineal gland or a point in space, but the work which you are doing every day; and your object in thus concentrating is to be able to do your work with smooth rapidity and consummate skill; for until you can thus do your work, you have not gained any degree of control over the mind; you have not acquired the power of concentration.

This powerful focusing of one's thought and energy and will upon the doing of things is difficult at first as everything worth acquiring is difficult—but daily efforts, strenuously made and patiently followed up, will soon lead to such a measure of self-control as will enable one to bring a strong and penetrating mind to bear upon any work undertaken—a mind that will quickly comprehend all the details of the work and dispose of them with accuracy and dispatch.

You will thus, as your concentrative capacity increases, enlarge your usefulness in the scheme of things, and increase your value to the world, thus inviting nobler opportunities and opening the door to higher duties; you will also experience the joy of a wider and fuller life.

In the process of concentration there are the four following stages:

1. Attention

2. Contemplation

3. Abstraction

4. Activity in Repose

At first the thoughts are arrested, and the mind is fixed upon the object of concentration, which is the task in hand—this is *attention*. The mind is then roused into vigorous thought concerning the way of proceeding with the task—this is *contemplation*.

Protracted contemplation leads to a condition of mind in which the doors of the senses are all closed against the entrance of outside distractions, the thoughts being wrapped in, and solely and intensely centered upon, the work in hand—this is *abstraction*. The mind thus centered in profound cogitation reaches a state in which the maximum of work is accomplished with the minimum of friction—this is *activity in repose*.

Attention is the first stage in all successful work. Those who lack it fail in everything. Such are the lazy, the thoughtless, the indifferent and incompetent. When attention is followed by an awakening of the mind to serious thought, then the second stage is reached. To ensure success in all ordinary, worldly undertakings, it is not necessary to go beyond these two stages.

They are reached, in a greater or lesser degree, by all that large army of skilled and competent workers which carries out the work of the world in its manifold departments, and only a comparatively small number reach the third stage of *abstraction*; for when abstraction is reached, we have entered the sphere of genius.

In the first two stages, the work and the mind are separate, and the work is done more or less laboriously, and with a degree of friction; but in the third stage, a marriage of the work with the mind takes place, there is a fusion, a union, and the two become one. Then there is a superior efficiency with less labor and friction. In the perfection of the first two stages, the mind is objectively engaged and is easily drawn from its center by external sights and sounds; but when the mind has attained perfection in abstraction, the *subjective* method of working is accomplished, as distinguished from the *objective*.

The thinker is then oblivious to the outside world, but is vividly alive in their mental operations. If spoken to, they will not hear; and if plied with more vigorous appeals, they will bring back their mind to outside things as one coming out of a dream; indeed, this abstraction is a kind of waking dream, but its similarity to a dream ends with the subjective state. It does not obtain in the mental operations of that state, in which, instead of the confusion of dreaming, there is perfect order, penetrating insight, and a wide range of comprehension. Whoever attains to perfection in abstraction will manifest genius in the particular work upon which their mind is centered.

Inventors, artists, poets, scientists, philosophers, and all people of genius are people of abstraction. They accomplish subjectively, and with ease, that which the objective workers—those who have not yet attained beyond the second stage in concentration—cannot accomplish with the most strenuous labor.

When the fourth stage—that of *activity in repose*—is attained, then concentration in its perfection is acquired. I am unable to find a single word which will fully express this dual condition of intense activity combined with steadiness, or rest, and have therefore employed the term "activity in repose."

The term appears contradictory, but the simple illustration of a spinning top will serve to explain the paradox. When a top spins at the maximum velocity, the friction is reduced to the minimum, and the top assumes that condition of perfect repose which is a sight so beautiful to the eye, and so captivating to the mind, of the schoolboy, who then says his top is "asleep."

The top is apparently motionless, but it is the rest, not of inertia, but of intense and perfectly balanced activity. So the mind that has acquired perfect concentration is, when engaged in that intense activity of thought which results in productive work of the highest kind, in a state of quiet poise and calm repose. Externally, there is no apparent activity, no disturbance, and the face of a person who has acquired this power will assume a more or less radiant calmness, and the face will be more sublimely calm when the mind is most intensely engaged in active thought.

Each stage of concentration has its particular power. Thus the first stage, when perfected, leads to usefulness; the second leads to skill, ability, talent; the third leads to originality and genius; while the fourth leads to mastery and power, and makes leaders and teachers of men.

In the development of concentration, also, as in all objects of growth, the following stages embody the preceding ones in their entirety. Thus in contemplation, attention is contained; in abstraction, both attention and contemplation are embodied; and one who has reached the last stage brings into play, in the act of contemplation, all the four stages.

Those who have perfected themselves in concentration are able, at any moment, to bring their thoughts to a point upon any matter, and to search into it with the strong light of an active comprehension. They can both take a thing up and lay it down with equal deliberation. They have learned how to use their thinking faculties to fixed purposes, and guide them toward definite ends. They are intelligent doers of things, and not weak wanderers amid chaotic thought.

Decision, energy, alertness, as well as deliberation, judgment, and gravity, accompany the habit of concentration; and that vigorous mental training which its cultivation involves, leads, through ever increasing usefulness and success in worldly occupations, toward that higher form of concentration called "meditation," in which the mind becomes divinely illumined and acquires the heavenly knowledge.

CHAPTER 8

Practice of Meditation

When *aspiration* is united to *concentration*, the result is *meditation*. When a person intensely desires to reach and realize a higher, purer, and more radiant life than the merely worldly and pleasure loving life, they engage in *aspiration*; and when they earnestly concentrate their thoughts upon the finding of that life, they practice meditation.

Without intense aspiration, there can be no meditation. Lethargy and indifference are fatal to its practice. The more intense the nature of a person, the more readily will they find meditation, and the more successfully will they practice it. A fiery nature will most rapidly scale the heights of truth in meditation when its aspirations have become sufficiently awakened.

Concentration is necessary to worldly success; meditation is necessary to spiritual success. Worldly skill and knowledge are acquired by concentration; spiritual skill and knowledge are acquired by meditation. By concentration a person can scale the highest heights of genius, but they cannot scale the heavenly heights of truth; to accomplish this, they must meditate.

By concentration a person may acquire the wonderful comprehension and vast power of a Caesar; by meditation they may reach the divine wisdom and perfect peace of a Buddha. The perfection of concentration is power; the perfection of meditation is *wisdom*.

By concentration, individuals acquire *skill* in the doing of the things of life—in science, art, trade, etc.—but by meditation, they acquire skill in *life itself*—in right living, enlightenment, wisdom, etc. Saints, sages, saviors—wise people and divine teachers—are the finished products of holy meditation.

The four stages in concentration are brought into play in meditation; the difference between the two powers being one of *direction* and not of nature. Meditation is therefore *spiritual concentration*—the bringing of the mind to a focus in its search for the divine knowledge, the divine life—the intense dwelling, in thought, on truth.

Thus a person aspires to know and realize, above all things else, the truth; they then give *attention* to conduct, to life, to self-purification. Giving attention to these things, they pass into serious *contemplation* of the facts, problems, and mystery of life. Thus contemplating, they come to love truth so fully and intensely as to become wholly absorbed in it, the mind is drawn away from its wanderings in a multitude of desires, and, solving one by one the problems of life, realizes that profound union with truth which is the state of abstraction. Thus absorbed in truth, there is that balance and poise of character, that divine *action in repose*, which is the abiding calm and peace of an emancipated and enlightened mind.

Meditation is more difficult to practice than concentration because it involves a much more severe self-discipline than that which obtains in concentration. A person can practice concentration without purifying their heart and life, whereas the process of purification is inseparable from meditation.

The object of meditation is divine enlightenment, the attainment of truth, and is therefore interwoven with practical purity and righteousness. Thus while, at first, the time spent in actual meditation is short—perhaps only half an hour in the early morning—the knowledge gained in that half hour of vivid aspiration and concentrated thought is embodied in practice during the whole day.

In meditation, therefore, the entire life of a person is involved; and as they advance in its practice they become more and more fitted to perform the duties of life in the circumstances in which they may be placed, for they become stronger, holier, calmer, and wiser. The principle of meditation is twofold, namely:

1. Purification of the heart by repetitive thought on pure things.

2. Attainment of divine knowledge by embodying such purity in practical life.

Man is a *thought being,* and his life and character are determined by the thoughts in which he habitually dwells. By practice, association, and habit, thoughts tend to repeat themselves with greater and greater ease and frequency, and so "fix" the character in a given direction by producing that automatic action which is called "habit."

By daily dwelling upon pure thoughts, the person of meditation forms the habit of pure and enlightened thinking which leads to pure and enlightened actions and well performed duties. By the ceaseless repetition of pure thoughts, they at last become one with those thoughts and are a purified being, manifesting their attainment in pure actions, in a serene and wise life.

The majority of people live in a series of conflicting desires, passions, emotions, and speculations, and there are restlessness, uncertainty, and sorrow; but when a person begins to train their mind in meditation, they gradually gain control over this inward conflict by bringing their thoughts to a focus upon a central principle.

In this way, the old habits of impure and erroneous thought and action are broken up, and the new habits of pure and enlightened thought and action are formed; the individual becomes more and more reconciled to truth, and there is increasing harmony and insight, a growing perfection and peace.

A powerful and lofty aspiration toward truth is always accompanied with a keen sense of the sorrow and brevity and mystery of life, and until this condition of mind is reached, meditation is impossible. Merely musing or whiling away the time in idle dreaming, habits to which the word *meditation* is frequently applied, are very far removed from meditation, in the lofty spiritual sense which we attach to that condition.

It is easy to mistake reverie for meditation. This is a fatal error which must be avoided by one striving to meditate. The two must not be confounded. Reverie is a loose dreaming into which a person falls; meditation is a strong, purposeful thinking into which a person rises. Reverie is easy and pleasurable; meditation is at first difficult and irksome.

Reverie thrives in indolence and luxury; meditation arises from strenuousness and discipline. Reverie is first alluring, then sensuous, and then sensual. Meditation is first forbidding, then profitable, and then peaceful. Reverie is dangerous; it undermines self-control. Meditation is protective; it establishes self-control.

There are certain signs by which one can know whether they are engaging in reverie or meditation.

THE INDICATIONS OF REVERIE ARE:

1. A desire to avoid exertion.
2. A desire to experience the pleasures of dreaming.

3. An increasing distaste for one's worldly duties.

4. A desire to shirk one's worldly responsibilities.

5. Fear of consequences.

6. A wish to get money with as little effort as possible.

7. Lack of self-control.

THE INDICATIONS OF MEDITATION ARE:

1. Increase of both physical and mental energy.

2. A strenuous striving after wisdom.

3. A decrease of irksomeness in the performance of duty.

4. A fixed determination to faithfully fulfill all worldly responsibilities.

5. Freedom from fear.

6. Indifference to riches.

7. Possession of self-control.

There are certain times, places, and conditions in and under which it is impossible to meditate; others wherein it is difficult to meditate; and others wherein meditation is rendered more accessible; and these, which should be known and carefully observed, are as follows:

TIMES, PLACES, AND CONDITIONS IN WHICH MEDITATION IS IMPOSSIBLE:

1. At, or immediately after, meals.

2. In places of pleasure.

3. In crowded places.

4. While walking rapidly.
5. While lying in bed in the morning.
6. While smoking.
7. While lying on a couch or bed for physical or mental relaxation.

TIMES, PLACES, AND CONDITIONS IN WHICH MEDITATION IS DIFFICULT:

1. At night.
2. In a luxuriously furnished room.
3. While sitting on a soft, yielding seat.
4. While wearing fancy clothing.
5. When in company.
6. When the body is weary.

7. If the body is given too much food.

TIMES, PLACES, AND CONDITIONS IN WHICH IT IS BEST TO MEDITATE:

1. Very early in the morning.
2. Immediately before meals.
3. In solitude.
4. In the open air or in a plainly furnished room.
5. While sitting on a hard seat.
6. When the body is strong and vigorous.
7. When the body is modestly and plainly clothed.

It will be seen by the foregoing instructions that ease, luxury, and indulgence (which induce reverie) render meditation difficult, and when strongly pronounced make it impossible; while strenuousness, discipline, and self-denial (which dispel reverie) make meditation comparatively easy. The body, too, should be neither overfed nor starved; neither in rags nor flauntingly clothed. It should not be tired, but should be at its highest point of energy and strength, as the holding of the mind to a concentrated train of subtle and lofty thought requires a high degree of both physical and mental energy.

Aspiration can often best be aroused and the mind renewed in meditation by the mental repetition of a lofty precept, a beautiful sentence, or a verse of poetry. Indeed, the mind that is ready for meditation will instinctively adopt this practice. Mere mechanical repetition is worthless, and even a hindrance.

The words repeated must be so applicable to one's own condition that they are dwelt upon lovingly and with concentrated devotion. In this way aspiration and concentration harmoniously combine to produce, without undue strain, the state of meditation. All the conditions above stated are of the utmost importance in the early stages of meditation and should be carefully noted and duly observed by all who are striving to acquire the practice. Those who faithfully follow the instructions and who strive and persevere will not fail to gather in, in due season, the harvest of purity, wisdom, bliss, and peace, and will surely eat of the sweet fruits of holy meditation.

CHAPTER 9

The Power of Purpose

Dispersion is weakness; concentration is power. Destruction is a scattering; preservation a uniting process. Things are useful and thoughts are powerful in the measure that their parts are strongly and intelligently concentrated. Purpose is highly concentrated thought.

All the mental energies are directed to the attainment of an object, and obstacles which intervene between the thinker and the object are, one after another, broken down and overcome. Purpose is the keystone in the temple of achievement. It binds and holds together in a complete whole that which would otherwise lie scattered and useless.

Empty whims, ephemeral fancies, vague desires, and half-hearted resolutions have no place in purpose. In the sustained determination to accomplish there is an invincible power which swallows up all inferior considerations and marches direct to victory.

All successful individuals are people of purpose. They hold fast to an idea, a project, a plan, and will not let it go; they cherish it, brood upon it, tend and develop it; and when assailed by difficulties, they refuse to be beguiled into surrender; indeed, the intensity of the purpose increases with the growing magnitude of the obstacles encountered.

The people who have molded the destinies of humanity have been people mighty of purpose. Like the Roman laying a road, they have followed along a well defined path and have refused to swerve aside even when torture and death confronted them. The great leaders of the race are the mental road makers, and mankind follows in the intellectual and spiritual paths which they have carved out and beaten.

Great is the power of purpose. To know how great, let a person study it in the lives of those whose influence has shaped the ends of nations and directed the destinies of the world. In an Alexander, a Caesar, or a Napoleon, we see the power of purpose when it is directed in worldly and personal channels; in a Confucius, a Buddha, or a

Christ, we perceive its vaster power when its course is along heavenly and impersonal paths.

Purpose goes with intelligence. There are lesser and greater purposes according with degrees of intelligence. A great mind will always be great of purpose. A weak intelligence will be without purpose. A drifting mind argues a measure of undevelopment.

What can resist an unshakable purpose? What can stand against it or turn it aside? Inert matter yields to a living force, and circumstance succumbs to the power of purpose. Truly, the person of unlawful purpose will, in achieving their ends, destroy themselves, but the person of good and lawful purpose cannot fail. It only needs that they daily renew the fire and energy of their fixed resolve to consummate their object.

The weak person, who grieves because they are misunderstood, will not greatly achieve; the vain person, who steps aside from their resolve in order to please others and gain their approbation, will not highly achieve; the double minded person, who thinks to compromise their purpose, will fail.

The person of fixed purpose who, whether misunderstandings and foul accusations or flatteries and fair promises rain upon him, does not yield a fraction of their resolve, is the person of excellence and achievement—of success, greatness, power.

Hindrances stimulate the person of purpose; difficulties nerve them to renewed exertion; mistakes, losses, pains, do not subdue them; and failures are steps in the ladder of success, for they are ever conscious of the certainty of final achievement.

All things at last yield to the silent, irresistible, all conquering energy of purpose.

> *"Out of the night that covers me,*
> *Black as the pit from pole to pole,*
> *I thank whatever gods may be*
> *For my unconquerable soul.*
> *In the fell clutch of circumstance*
> *I have not whined nor cried aloud;*
> *Under the bludgeoning of chance*
> *My head is bloody but unbowed.*
> *It matters not how strait the gate,*
> *How charged with punishment the scroll;*
> *I am the master of my fate,*
> *I am the captain of my soul."*
>
> —William Ernest Henley, "Invictus"

CHAPTER 10

The Joy of Accomplishment

Joy is always the accompaniment of a task successfully accomplished. An undertaking completed, or a piece of work done, always brings rest and satisfaction. "When a man has done his duty, he is light-hearted and happy," says Emerson; and no matter how insignificant the task may appear, the doing of it faithfully and with whole-souled energy always results in cheerfulness and peace of mind.

Of all miserable people, the shirker is the most miserable. Thinking to find ease and happiness in avoiding difficult duties and necessary tasks, which require the expenditure of labor and exertion, their mind is always uneasy and disturbed. They become burdened with an inward sense of shame, and forfeit self-respect.

"He who will not work according to his faculty, let him perish according to his necessity," says Carlyle; and it is a moral law that the person who avoids duty and does not work to the full extent of their capacity does actually perish, first in their character and last in their body and circumstances. Life and action are synonymous, and immediately a person tries to escape exertion, either physical or mental, they have commenced to decay.

On the other hand, the energetic people increase in life by the full exercise of their powers, by overcoming difficulties, and by bringing to completion tasks which coiled for the strenuous use of mind or muscle.

How happy is a child when a school lesson, long labored over, is mastered at last! The athlete, who has trained their body through long months or years of discipline and strain, is richly blessed in their increased health and strength and is met with the rejoicings of their friends when they carry home the prize from the field of contest. After many years of ungrudging toil, the heart of the scholar is gladdened with the advantages and powers which learning bestows.

The businessperson, grappling incessantly with difficulties and drawbacks, is amply repaid in the happy assurance of well earned success; and the horticulturist, vigorously contending with the stubborn soil, sits down at last to eat of the fruits of their labor.

Every successful accomplishment, even in worldly things, is repaid with its own measure of joy; and in spiritual things, the joy which supervenes upon the perfection of purpose is sure, deep, and abiding. Great is the heartfelt joy (albeit ineffable) when, after innumerable and apparently unsuccessful attempts, some ingrained fault of character is at last cast out to trouble its erstwhile victim and the world no more.

The striver after virtue—one who is engaged in the holy task of building up a noble character—tastes, at every step of conquest over self, a joy which does not again leave them, but which becomes an integral part of their spiritual nature.

All life is a struggle; both without and within there are conditions against which individuals must contend. Their very existence is a series of efforts and accomplishments, and their right to remain among others as a useful unit of humanity depends upon the measure of their capacity for wrestling successfully with the elements of nature without, or with the enemies of virtue and truth within.

It is demanded of each that they shall continue to strive after better things, after greater perfection, after higher and still higher achievements; and in accordance with the measure of their obedience to this demand does the angel of joy wait upon their footsteps and minister unto them; for one who is anxious to learn, eager to know, and who puts forth efforts to accomplish, finds the joy which eternally sings at the heart of the universe.

First in little things, then in greater, and then in greater still, must people strive; until at last they are prepared to make the supreme effort and strive for the accomplishment of truth, succeeding in which, they will realize the eternal joy.

The price of life is effort; the acme of effort is accomplishment; the reward of accomplishment is joy. Blessed is the one who strives against their own selfishness; they will taste in its fullness the joy of accomplishment.

The Path of Prosperity

James Allen

What you are, so is your world.

CHAPTER 1

The Lesson of Evil

Unrest and pain and sorrow are the shadows of life. There is no heart in all the world that has not felt the sting of pain, no mind has not been tossed upon the dark waters of trouble, no eye that has not wept the hot blinding tears of unspeakable anguish.

There is no household where the Great Destroyers, disease and death, have not entered, severing heart from heart, and casting over all the dark pall of sorrow. In the strong and apparently indestructible meshes of evil all are more or less fast caught, and pain, unhappiness, and misfortune wait upon humankind.

With the object of escaping, or in some way mitigating this overshadowing gloom, men and women rush blindly into innumerable devices, pathways by which they fondly hope to enter into a happiness which will not pass away.

Such are the drunkard and the harlot, who revel in sensual excitements; such is the exclusive aesthete, who shuts himself out from the sorrows of the world, and surrounds himself with enervating luxuries; such is he who thirsts for wealth or fame, and subordinates all things to the achievement of that object; and such are they who seek consolation in the performance of religious rites.

And to all the happiness sought seems to come, and the soul, for a time, is lulled into a sweet security, and an intoxicating forgetfulness of the existence of evil; but the day of disease comes at last, or some great sorrow, temptation, or misfortune breaks suddenly in on the unfortified soul, and the fabric of its fancied happiness is torn to shreds.

So over the head of every personal joy hangs the Damocletian sword of pain, ready, at any moment, to fall and crush the soul of him who is unprotected by knowledge.

The child cries to be a man or woman; the man and woman sigh for the lost felicity of childhood. The poor man chafes under the chains of poverty by which he is bound, and the rich man often lives in fear of poverty, or scours the world in search of an elusive shadow he calls happiness.

Sometimes the soul feels that it has found a secure peace and happiness in adopting a certain religion, in embracing an intellectual philosophy, or in building up an intellectual or artistic ideal; but some overpowering temptation proves the religion to be inadequate or insufficient; the theoretical philosophy is found to be a useless prop; or in a moment, the idealistic statue, upon which the devotee has for years been laboring, is shattered into fragments at his feet.

Is there, then, no way of escape from pain and sorrow? Are there no means by which bonds of evil may be broken? Is permanent happiness, secure prosperity, and abiding peace a foolish dream?

No, there is a way, and I speak it with gladness, by which evil can be slain forever; there is a process by which disease, poverty, or any adverse condition or circumstance can be put on one side never to return; there is a method by which a permanent prosperity can be secured, free from all fear of the return of adversity, and there is a practice by which unbroken and unending peace and bliss can be partaken of and realized.

And the beginning of the way which leads to this glorious realization is the acquirement of a right understanding of the nature of evil.

It is not sufficient to deny or ignore evil; it must be understood. It is not enough to pray to God to remove the evil; you must find out why it is there, and what lesson it has for you.

It is of no avail to fret and fume and chafe at the chains which bind you; you must know why and how you are bound. Therefore, reader, you must get outside yourself, and must begin to examine and understand yourself.

You must cease to be a disobedient child in the school of experience and must begin to learn, with humility and patience, the lessons that are set for your edification and ultimate perfection; for evil, when rightly understood, is found to be, not an unlimited power or principle in the universe, but a passing phase of human experience, and it therefore becomes a teacher to those who are willing to learn.

Evil is not an abstract something outside yourself; it is an experience in your own heart, and by patiently examining and rectifying your heart you will be gradually led into the discovery of the origin and nature of evil, which will necessarily be followed by its complete eradication.

All evil is corrective and remedial, and is therefore not permanent. It is rooted in ignorance, ignorance of the true nature and relation of things, and so long as we remain in that state of ignorance, we remain subject to evil.

There is no evil in the universe which is not the result of ignorance, and which would not, if we were ready and willing to learn its lesson, lead us to higher wisdom, and then vanish away. But people remain in evil, and it does not pass away because people are not willing or prepared to learn the lesson which it came to teach them.

I knew a child who, every night when its mother took it to bed, cried to be allowed to play with the candle; and one night, when the mother was off guard for a moment, the child took hold of the candle; the inevitable result followed, and the child never wished to play with the candle again.

By its one foolish act it learned, and learned perfectly, the lesson of obedience, and entered into the knowledge that fire burns. This incident is a complete illustration of the nature, meaning, and ultimate result of all sin and evil.

As the child suffered through its own ignorance of the real nature of fire, so older children suffer through their ignorance of the real nature of the things which they weep for and strive after, and which harm them when they are secured; the only difference being that in the latter case the ignorance and evil are more deeply rooted and obscure.

Evil has always been symbolized by darkness, and Good by light, and hidden within the symbol is contained the perfect interpretation, the reality; for, just as light always floods the universe, and darkness is only a mere speck or shadow cast by a small body intercepting a few rays of the illimitable light, so the Light of the Supreme Good is the positive and life-giving power which floods the universe, and evil the insignificant shadow cast by the self that intercepts and shuts off the illuminating rays which strive for entrance.

When night folds the world in its black impenetrable mantle, no matter how dense the darkness, it covers but the small space of half our little planet, while the whole universe is ablaze with living light, and every soul knows that it will awake in the light in the morning.

Know, then, that when the dark night of sorrow, pain, or misfortune settles down upon your soul, and you stumble along with weary and uncertain steps, that you are merely intercepting your own personal desires between yourself and the boundless light of joy and bliss, and the dark shadow that covers you is cast by none and nothing but yourself.

And just as the darkness without is but a negative shadow, an unreality which comes from nowhere, goes to nowhere, and has no abiding dwelling place, so the darkness within is equally a negative shadow passing over the evolving and Lightborn soul.

"But," I fancy I hear someone say, "why pass through the darkness of evil at all?" Because, by ignorance, you have chosen to do so, and because, by doing so, you may understand both good and evil, and may the more appreciate the light by having passed through the darkness.

As evil is the direct outcome of ignorance, so, when the lessons of evil are fully learned, ignorance passes away, and wisdom takes its place. But as a disobedient child refuses to learn its lessons at school, so it is possible to refuse to learn the lessons of experience, and thus to remain in continual darkness and to suffer continually recurring punishments in the form of disease, disappointment, and sorrow.

He, therefore, who would shake himself free of the evil which encompasses him must be willing and ready to learn, and must be prepared to undergo that disciplinary process without which no grain of wisdom or abiding happiness and peace can be secured.

A person may shut themselves up in a dark room, and deny that the light exists, but it is everywhere without, and darkness exists only in their own little room.

So you may shut out the light of Truth, or you may begin to pull down the walls of prejudice, self-seeking, and error which you have built around yourself, and so let in the glorious and omnipresent Light.

By earnest self-examination strive to realize, and not merely hold as a theory, that evil is a passing phase, a self-created shadow; that all your pains, sorrows, and misfortunes have come to you by a process of undeviating and absolutely perfect law; have come to you because you deserve and require them, and that by first enduring, and then understanding them, you may be made stronger, wiser, nobler.

When you have fully entered into this realization, you will be in a position to mold your own circumstances, to transmute all evil into good and to weave, with a master hand, the fabric of your destiny.

What of the night, O Watchman! see'st thou yet
The glimmering dawn upon the mountain heights,
The golden Herald of the Light of lights,
Are his fair feet upon the hilltops set?

Cometh he yet to chase away the gloom,
And with it all the demons of the Night?
Strike yet his darting rays upon thy sight?

Hear'st thou his voice, the sound of error's doom?

The Morning cometh, lover of the Light;
Even now He gilds with gold the mountain's brow,
Dimly I see the path whereon even now
His shining feet are set toward the Night.

Darkness shall pass away, and all the things
That love the darkness, and that hate the Light
Shall disappear for ever with the Night:
Rejoice! for thus the speeding Herald sings.

CHAPTER 2

The World a Reflex of Mental States

What you are, so is your world. Everything in the universe is resolved into your own inward experience. It matters little what is without, for it is all a reflection of your own state of consciousness.

It matters everything what you are within, for everything without will be mirrored and colored accordingly.

All that you positively know is contained in your own experience; all that you ever will know must pass through the gateway of experience, and so become part of yourself.

Your own thoughts, desires, and aspirations comprise your world, and, to you, all that there is in the universe of beauty and joy and bliss, or of ugliness and sorrow and pain, is contained within yourself.

By your own thoughts you make or mar your life, your world, your universe. As you build within by the power of thought, so will your outward life and circumstances shape themselves accordingly.

Whatsoever you harbor in the inmost chambers of your heart will, sooner or later by the inevitable law of reaction, shape itself in your outward life.

The soul that is impure, sordid, and selfish is gravitating with unerring precision toward misfortune and catastrophe; the soul that is pure, unselfish, and noble is gravitating with equal precision toward happiness and prosperity.

Every soul attracts its own, and nothing can possibly come to it that does not belong to it. To realize this is to recognize the universality of Divine Law.

The incidents of every human life, which both make and mar, are drawn to it by the quality and power of its own inner thought-life. Every soul is a complex combination of gathered experiences and thoughts, and the body is but an improvised vehicle for its manifestation.

What, therefore, your thoughts are, that is your real self; and the world around, both animate and inanimate, wears the aspect with which your thoughts clothe it.

"All that we are is the result of what we have thought. It is founded on our thoughts; it is made up of our thoughts." Thus said Buddha, and it therefore follows that if a person is happy, it is because they dwell in happy thoughts; if miserable, because they dwell in despondent and debilitating thoughts,

Whether one be fearful or fearless, foolish or wise, troubled or serene, within that soul lies the cause of its own state or states, and never without. And now I seem to hear a chorus of voices exclaim, "But do you really mean to say that outward circumstances do not affect our minds?" I do not say that, but I say this, and know it to be an infallible truth, that circumstances can only affect you in so far as you allow them to do so.

You are swayed by circumstances because you have not a right understanding of the nature, use, and power of thought.

You believe (and upon this little word belief hang all our sorrows and joys) that outward things have the power to make or mar your life. By so doing you submit to those outward things, confess that you are their slave, and they your unconditional master. By so doing, you invest them with a power which they do not, of themselves, possess, and you succumb, in reality, not to the mere circumstances, but to the gloom or gladness, the fear or hope, the strength or weakness, which your thought-sphere has thrown around them.

I knew two men who, at an early age, lost the hard-earned savings of years. One was very deeply troubled, and gave way to chagrin, worry, and despondency.

The other, on reading in his morning paper that the bank in which his money was deposited had hopelessly failed, and that he had lost all, quietly and firmly remarked, "Well, it's gone, and trouble and worry won't bring it back, but hard work will."

He went to work with renewed vigor, and rapidly became prosperous, while the former man, continuing to mourn the loss of his money and to grumble at his "bad luck," remained the sport and tool of adverse circumstances, in reality of his own weak and slavish thoughts.

The loss of money was a curse to the one because he clothed the event with dark and dreary thoughts; it was a blessing to the other, because he threw around it thoughts of strength, of hope, and renewed endeavor.

If circumstances had the power to bless or harm, they would bless and harm all people alike, but the fact that the same circumstances will be alike good and bad to different souls proves that the good or bad is not in the circumstance, but only in the mind of the one who encounters it.

When you begin to realize this you will begin to control your thoughts, to regulate and discipline your mind, and to rebuild the inward temple of your soul, eliminating all useless and superfluous material, and incorporating into your being thoughts alone of joy and serenity, of strength and life, of compassion and love, of beauty and immortality; and as you do this you will become joyful and serene, strong and healthy, compassionate and loving, and beautiful with the beauty of immortality.

And as we clothe events with the drapery of our own thoughts, so likewise do we clothe the objects of the visible world around us, and where one sees harmony and beauty, another sees revolting ugliness.

An enthusiastic naturalist was one day roaming the country lanes in pursuit of his hobby, and during his rambles came upon a pool of brackish water near a farmyard.

As he proceeded to fill a small bottle with the water for the purpose of examination under the microscope, he dilated, with more enthusiasm than discretion, to an uncultivated son of the plough who stood close by, upon the hidden and innumerable wonders contained in the pool, and concluded by saying, "Yes, my friend, within this pool is contained a hundred, nay, a million universes, had we but the sense or the instrument by which we could apprehend them." And the unsophisticated one ponderously remarked, "I know the water be full o' tadpoles, but they be easy to catch."

Where the naturalist, his mind stored with the knowledge of natural facts, saw beauty, harmony, and hidden glory, the mind unenlightened upon those things saw only an offensive mud-puddle.

The wild flower which the casual wayfarer thoughtlessly tramples upon is, to the spiritual eye of the poet, an angelic messenger from the invisible.

To the many, the ocean is but a dreary expanse of water on which ships sail and are sometimes wrecked; to the soul of the musician it is a living thing, and he hears, in all its changing moods, divine harmonies.

Where the ordinary mind sees disaster and confusion, the mind of the philosopher sees the most perfect sequence of cause and effect, and where the materialist sees nothing but endless death, the mystic sees pulsating and eternal life.

And as we clothe both events and objects with our own thoughts, so likewise do we clothe the souls of others in the garments of our thoughts.

The suspicious believe everybody to be suspicious; the liar feels secure in the thought that he is not so foolish as to believe that there is such a phenomenon as a strictly truthful person; the envious see envy in every soul; the miser thinks everybody is eager to get his money; he who has subordinated conscience in the making of his wealth sleeps with a revolver under his pillow, wrapped in the delusion that the world is full of conscienceless people who are eager to rob him, and the abandoned sensualist looks upon the saint as a hypocrite.

On the other hand, those who dwell in loving thoughts see that in all which calls forth their love and sympathy; the trusting and honest are not troubled by suspicions; the good-natured and charitable who rejoice at the good fortune of others scarcely know what envy means; and he who has realized the Divine within himself recognizes it in all beings, even in the beasts.

And men and women are confirmed in their mental outlook because of the fact that, by the law of cause and effect, they attract to themselves that which they send forth, and so come in contact with people similar to themselves.

The old adage, "Birds of a feather flock together," has a deeper significance than is generally attached to it, for in the thought-world as in the world of matter, each clings to its kind.

Do you wish for kindness? Be kind.
Do you ask for truth? Be true.
What you give of yourself you find;
Your world is a reflex of you.

If you are one of those who are praying for, and looking forward to, a happier world beyond the grave, here is a message of gladness for you—you may enter into and realize that happy world now; it fills the whole universe, and it is within you, waiting for you to find, acknowledge, and possess.

Said one who knew the inner laws of Being: "When men shall say lo here, or lo there, go not after them; the kingdom of God is within you."

What you have to do is to believe this, simply believe it with a mind unshadowed by doubt, and then meditate upon it till you understand it.

You will then begin to purify and to build your inner world, and as you proceed, passing from revelation to revelation, from realization to realization, you will discover the utter powerlessness of outward things beside the magic potency of a self-governed soul.

If thou would'st right the world,
And banish all its evils and its woes,
Make its wild places bloom,
And its drear deserts blossom as the rose—
Then right thyself.

If thou would'st turn the world
From its long, lone captivity in sin,
Restore all broken hearts,
Slay grief, and let sweet consolation in—
Turn thou thyself.

If thou would'st cure the world
Of its long sickness, end its grief and pain;
Bring in all-healing joy,
And give to the afflicted rest again—
Then cure thyself.

If thou would'st wake the world
Out of its dream of death and dark'ning strife,
Bring it to Love and Peace,

And Light and brightness of immortal Life—
Wake thou thyself.

CHAPTER 3

The Way Out of Undesirable Conditions

Having seen and realized that evil is but a passing shadow thrown, by the intercepting self, across the transcendent Form of the Eternal Good, and that the world is a mirror in which each sees a reflection of himself, we now ascend, by firm and easy steps, to that plane of perception whereon is seen and realized the Vision of the Law.

With this realization comes the knowledge that everything is included in a ceaseless interaction of cause and effect, and that nothing can possibly be divorced from law.

From the most trivial thought, word, or act, up to the groupings of the celestial bodies, law reigns supreme. No arbitrary condition can, even for one moment, exist, for such a condition would be a denial and an annihilation of law.

Every condition of life is, therefore, bound up in an orderly and harmonious sequence, and the secret and cause of every condition is contained within itself, The law, "Whatsoever a man sows that shall he also reap," is inscribed in flaming letters upon the portal of Eternity, and none can deny it, none can cheat it, none can escape it.

He who puts his hand in the fire must suffer the burning until such time as it has worked itself out, and neither curses nor prayers can avail to alter it.

And precisely the same law governs the realm of mind. Hatred, anger, jealousy, envy, lust, covetousness, all these are fires which burn, and whoever even so much as touches them must suffer the torments of burning.

All these conditions of mind are rightly called "evil," for they are the efforts of the soul to subvert, in its ignorance, the law, and they, therefore, lead to chaos and confusion within, and are sooner or later actualized in the outward circumstances as disease, failure, and misfortune, coupled with grief, pain, and despair.

Whereas love, gentleness, goodwill, and purity are cooling airs which breathe peace upon the soul that does them, and, being in harmony with the Eternal Law, they become actualized in the form of health, peaceful surroundings, and undeviating success and good fortune.

A thorough understanding of this Great Law which permeates the universe leads to the acquirement of that state of mind known as obedience.

To know that justice, harmony, and love are supreme in the universe is likewise to know that all adverse and painful conditions are the result of our own disobedience to that Law.

Such knowledge leads to strength and power, and it is upon such knowledge alone that a true life and an enduring success and happiness can be built.

To be patient under all circumstances, and to accept all conditions as necessary factors in your training, is to rise superior to all painful conditions, and to overcome them with an overcoming which is sure, and which leaves no fear of their return, for by the power of obedience to law they are utterly slain.

Such an obedient one is working in harmony with the law—has in fact, identified himself with the law—and whatsoever he conquers he conquers forever; whatsoever he builds can never be destroyed.

The cause of all power, as of all weakness, is within; the secret of all happiness, as of all misery, is likewise within.

There is no progress apart from unfoldment within, and no sure foothold of prosperity or peace except by orderly advancement in knowledge.

You say you are chained by circumstances; you cry out for better opportunities, for a wider scope, for improved physical conditions, and perhaps you inwardly curse the fate that binds you hand and foot.

It is for you that I write; it is to you that I speak. Listen, and let my words burn themselves into your heart, for that which I say to you is truth:

You may bring about that improved condition in your outward life which you desire if you will unswervingly resolve to improve your inner life.

I know this pathway looks barren at its commencement (truth always does, it is only error and delusion which are at first inviting and fascinating). But if you undertake to walk it, if you perseveringly discipline your mind, eradicating your weaknesses, and allowing your soul-forces and spiritual powers to unfold themselves, you will be astonished at the magical changes which will be brought about in your outward life.

As you proceed, golden opportunities will be strewn across your path, and the power and judgment to properly utilize them will spring up within you. Genial friends will come unbidden to you; sympathetic souls will be drawn to you as the needle is to the magnet; and books and all outward aids that you require will come to you unsought.

Perhaps the chains of poverty hang heavily upon you, and you are friendless and alone, and you long with an intense longing that your load may be lightened; but the load continues, and you seem to be enveloped in an ever-increasing darkness.

Perhaps you complain, you bewail your lot; you blame your birth, your parents, your employer, or the unjust Powers who have bestowed upon you so undeservedly poverty and hardship, and upon another affluence and ease.

Cease your complaining and fretting; none of these things which you blame are the cause of your poverty; the cause is within yourself, and where the cause is, there is the remedy.

The very fact that you are a complainer shows that you deserve your lot; shows that you lack that faith which is the ground of all effort and progress.

There is no room for a complainer in a universe of law, and worry is soul-suicide. By your very attitude of mind you are strengthening the chains which bind you, and are drawing about you the darkness by which you are enveloped. Alter your outlook upon life, and your outward life will alter.

Build yourself up in faith and knowledge, and make yourself worthy of better surroundings and wider opportunities. Be sure, first of all, that you are making the best of what you have.

Do not delude yourself into supposing that you can step into greater advantages while overlooking smaller ones, for if you could, the advantage would be impermanent, and you would quickly fall back again in order to learn the lesson which you had neglected.

As the child at school must master one standard before passing on to the next, so, before you can have that greater good which you so desire, must you faithfully employ that which you already possess.

The parable of the talents is a beautiful story illustrative of this truth, for does it not plainly show that if we misuse, neglect, or degrade that which we possess, be it ever so mean and insignificant, even that little will be taken from us? For by our conduct we show that we are unworthy of it.

Perhaps you are living in a small cottage, and are surrounded by unhealthy and vicious influences.

You desire a larger and more sanitary residence. Then you must fit yourself for such a residence by first of all making your cottage as far as possible a little paradise. Keep it spotlessly clean. Make it look as pretty and sweet as your limited means will allow. Cook your plain food with all care, and arrange your humble table as tastefully as you possibly can.

If you cannot afford a carpet, let your rooms be carpeted with smiles and welcomes, fastened down with the nails of kind words driven in with the hammer of patience. Such a carpet will not fade in the sun, and constant use will never wear it away.

By so ennobling your present surroundings you will rise above them, and above the need of them, and at the right time you will pass on into the better house and surroundings which have all along been waiting for you, and which you have fitted yourself to occupy.

Perhaps you desire more time for thought and effort, and feel that your hours of labor are too hard and long.

Then see to it that you are utilizing to the fullest possible extent what little spare time you have.

It is useless to desire more time, if you are already wasting what little you have; for you would only grow more indolent and indifferent.

Even poverty and lack of time and leisure are not the evils that you imagine they are, and if they hinder you in your progress, it is because you have clothed them in your own weaknesses, and the evil that you see in them is really in yourself. Endeavor to fully and completely realize that in so far as you shape and mold your mind, you are the maker of your destiny, and as, by the transmuting power of self-discipline you realize this more and more, you will come to see that these so-called evils may be converted into blessings.

You will then utilize your poverty for the cultivation of patience, hope, and courage; and your lack of time in the gaining of promptness of action and decision of mind, by seizing the precious moments as they present themselves for your acceptance.

As in the rankest soil the most beautiful flowers are grown, so in the dark soil of poverty the choicest flowers of humanity have developed and bloomed.

Where there are difficulties to cope with, and unsatisfactory conditions to overcome, there virtue most flourishes and manifests its glory.

It may be that you are in the employ of a tyrannous master or mistress, and you feel that you are harshly treated. Look upon this also as necessary to your training. Return your employer's unkindness with gentleness and forgiveness.

Practice unceasing patience and self-control. Turn the disadvantage to account by utilizing it for the gaining of mental and spiritual strength, and by your silent example and influence you will thus be teaching your employer, will be helping him to grow ashamed of his conduct, and will, at the same time, be lifting yourself up to that height of spiritual attainment by which you will be enabled to step into new and more congenial surroundings at the time when they are presented to you.

Do not complain that you are a slave, but lift yourself up, by noble conduct, above the plane of slavery. Before complaining that you are a slave to another, be sure that you are not a slave to self.

Look within; look searchingly, and have no mercy upon yourself. You will find there, perchance, slavish thoughts, slavish desires, and in your daily life and conduct slavish habits.

Conquer these; cease to be a slave to self, and no man will have the power to enslave you. As you overcome self, you will overcome all adverse conditions, and every difficulty will fall before you.

Do not complain that you are oppressed by the rich. Are you sure that if you gained riches you would not be an oppressor yourself?

Remember that there is the Eternal Law which is absolutely just, and that he who oppresses today must himself be oppressed tomorrow; and from this there is no way of escape.

And perhaps you, yesterday (in some former existence) were rich and an oppressor, and that you are now merely paying off the debt which you owe to the Great Law. Practice, therefore, fortitude and faith.

Dwell constantly in mind upon the Eternal justice, the Eternal Good. Endeavor to lift yourself above the personal and the transitory into the impersonal and permanent.

Shake off the delusion that you are being injured or oppressed by another, and try to realize, by a profounder comprehension of your inner life, and the laws which govern that life, that you are only really injured by what is within you. There is no practice more degrading, debasing, and soul-destroying than that of self-pity.

Cast it out from you. While such a canker is feeding upon your heart you can never expect to grow into a fuller life.

Cease from the condemnation of others, and begin to condemn yourself. Condone none of your acts, desires, or thoughts that will not bear comparison with spotless purity or endure the light of sinless good.

By so doing you will be building your house upon the rock of the Eternal, and all that is required for your happiness and well-being will come to you in its own time.

There is positively no way of permanently rising above poverty, or any undesirable condition, except by eradicating those selfish and negative conditions within, of which these are the reflection, and by virtue of which they continue.

The way to true riches is to enrich the soul by the acquisition of virtue. Outside of real heart-virtue there is neither prosperity nor power, but only the appearances of these. I am aware that men make money who have acquired no measure of virtue, and have little desire to do so; but such money does not constitute true riches, and its possession is transitory and feverish.

Here is David's testimony: "For I was envious at the foolish when I saw the prosperity of the wicked... Their eyes stand out with fatness; they have more than heart could wish. Verily I have cleansed my heart in vain, and washed my hands in innocence... When I thought to know this it was too painful for me; until I went into the sanctuary of God, then understood I their end."

The prosperity of the wicked was a great trial to David until he went into the sanctuary of God, and then he knew their end.

You likewise may go into that sanctuary. It is within you. It is that state of consciousness which remains when all that is sordid, and personal, and impermanent is risen above, and universal and eternal principles are realized.

That is the God state of consciousness; it is the sanctuary of the Most High. When by long strife and self-discipline you have succeeded in entering the door of that holy Temple, you will perceive, with unobstructed vision, the end and fruit of all human thought and endeavor, both good and evil.

You will then no longer relax your faith when you see the immoral man accumulating outward riches, for you will know that he must come again to poverty and degradation.

The rich man who is barren of virtue is, in reality, poor, and as surely as the waters of the river are drifting to the ocean, so surely is he, in the midst of all his riches, drifting toward poverty and misfortune; and though he die rich, yet must he return to reap the bitter fruit of all of his immorality.

And though he become rich many times, yet as many times must he be thrown back into poverty, until by long experience and suffering he conquers the poverty within.

But the man who is outwardly poor, yet rich in virtue, is truly rich, and in the midst of all his poverty he is surely traveling toward prosperity; and abounding joy and bliss await his coming. If you would become truly and permanently prosperous, you must first become virtuous.

It is therefore unwise to aim directly at prosperity, to make it the one object of life, to reach out greedily for it. To do this is to ultimately defeat yourself.

But rather aim at self-perfection, make useful and unselfish service the object of your life, and ever reach out hands of faith toward the supreme and unalterable Good.

You say you desire wealth, not for your own sake, but in order to do good with it and to bless others. If this is your real motive in desiring wealth, then wealth will come to you; for you are strong and unselfish indeed if, in the midst of riches, you are willing to look upon yourself as steward and not as owner.

But examine well your motive, for in the majority of instances where money is desired for the admitted object of blessing others, the real underlying motive is a love of popularity, and a desire to pose as a philanthropist or reformer.

If you are not doing good with what little you have, depend upon it the more money you got the more selfish you would become, and all the good you appeared to do with your money, if you attempted to do any, would be so much insinuating self-laudation.

If your real desire is to do good, there is no need to wait for money before you do it; you can do it now, this very moment, and just where you are. If you are really so unselfish as you believe yourself to be, you will show it by sacrificing yourself for others now.

No matter how poor you are, there is room for self-sacrifice, for did not the widow put her all into the treasury?

The heart that truly desires to do good does not wait for money before doing it, but comes to the altar of sacrifice and, leaving there the unworthy elements of self, goes out and breathes upon neighbor and stranger, friend and enemy alike the breath of blessedness.

As the effect is related to the cause, so is prosperity and power related to the inward good and poverty and weakness to the inward evil.

Money does not constitute true wealth, nor position, nor power, and to rely upon it alone is to stand upon a slippery place.

Your true wealth is your stock of virtue, and your true power the uses to which you put it. Rectify your heart, and you will rectify your life. Lust, hatred, anger, vanity, pride, covetousness, self-indulgence, self-seeking, obstinacy—all these are poverty and weakness; whereas love, purity, gentleness, meekness, compassion, generosity, self-forgetfulness, and self-renunciation—all these are wealth and power.

As the elements of poverty and weakness are overcome, an irresistible and all-conquering power is evolved from within, and one who succeeds in establishing themselves in the highest virtue brings the whole world to their feet.

But the rich, as well as the poor, have their undesirable conditions, and are frequently further removed from happiness than the poor. And here we see how happiness depends, not upon outward aids or possessions, but upon the inward life.

Perhaps you are an employer, and you have endless trouble with those whom you employ, and when you do get good and faithful servants they quickly leave you. As a result you are beginning to lose, or have completely lost, your faith in human nature.

You try to remedy matters by giving better wages and by allowing certain liberties, yet matters remain unaltered. Let me advise you.

The secret of all your trouble is not in your servants, it is in yourself; and if you look within, with a humble and sincere desire to discover and eradicate your error, you will, sooner or later, find the origin of all your unhappiness.

It may be some selfish desire, or lurking suspicion, or unkind attitude of mind which sends out its poison upon those about you and reacts upon yourself, even though you may not show it in your manner or speech.

Think of your servants with kindness, consider of them that extremity of service which you yourself would not care to perform were you in their place.

Rare and beautiful is that humility of soul by which a servant entirely forgets himself in his master's good; but far rarer, and beautiful with a divine beauty, is that nobility of soul by which a person, forgetting their own happiness, seeks the happiness of those who are under their authority and who depend upon them for their bodily sustenance.

Such a person's happiness is increased tenfold, nor do they need to complain of those whom they employ. Said a well-known and extensive employer of labor, who never needed to dismiss an employee: "I have always had the happiest relations with my workpeople. If you ask me how it is to be accounted for, I can only say that it has been my aim from the first to do to them as I would wish to be done by." Herein lies the secret by which all desirable conditions are secured, and all that are undesirable are overcome.

Do you say that you are lonely and unloved and have "not a friend in the world"? Then, I pray you, for the sake of your own happiness, blame nobody but yourself.

Be friendly toward others, and friends will soon flock round you. Make yourself pure and lovable, and you will be loved by all.

Whatever conditions are rendering your life burdensome, you may pass out of and beyond them by developing and utilizing within you the transforming power of self-purification and self-conquest.

Be it the poverty which galls (and remember that the poverty upon which I have been dilating is that poverty which is a source of misery, and not that voluntary poverty which is the glory of emancipated souls), or the riches which burden, or the many misfortunes, griefs, and annoyances which form the dark background in the web of life, you may overcome them by overcoming the selfish elements within which give them life.

It matters not that by the unfailing Law, there are past thoughts and acts to work out and to atone for, as, by the same law, we are setting in motion, during every moment of our life, fresh thoughts and acts, and we have the power to make them good or ill.

Nor does it follow that if a person (reaping what they have sown) must lose money or forfeit position, that they must also lose their fortitude or forfeit their uprightness, and it is in these that one's wealth and power and happiness are to be found. The one who clings to self is their own enemy and is surrounded by enemies.

The one who relinquishes self is their own savior, and is surrounded by friends like a protecting belt. Before the divine radiance of a pure heart all darkness vanishes and all clouds melt away, and one who has conquered self has conquered the universe.

Come, then, out of your poverty; come out of your pain; come out of your troubles, and sighings, and complainings, and heartaches, and loneliness by coming out of yourself.

Let the old tattered garment of your petty selfishness fall from you, and put on the new garment of universal Love. You will then realize the inward heaven, and it will be reflected in all your outward life.

He who sets his foot firmly upon the path of self-conquest, who walks, aided by the staff of Faith, the highway of self-sacrifice, will assuredly achieve the highest prosperity, and will reap abounding and enduring joy and bliss.

To them that seek the highest good
All things subserve the wisest ends;
Nought comes as ill, and wisdom lends
Wings to all shapes of evil brood.

The dark'ning sorrow veils a Star
That waits to shine with gladsome light;

Hell waits on heaven; and after night
Comes golden glory from afar.

Defeats are steps by which we climb
With purer aim to nobler ends;
Loss leads to gain, and joy attends
True footsteps up the hills of time.

Pain leads to paths of holy bliss,
To thoughts and words and deeds divine—
And clouds that gloom and rays that shine,
Along life's upward highway kiss.

Misfortune does but cloud the way
Whose end and summit in the sky
Of bright success, sunkiss'd and high,
Awaits our seeking and our stay.

The heavy pall of doubts and fears
That clouds the Valley of our hopes,
The shades with which the spirit copes,
The bitter harvesting of tears,

The heartaches, miseries, and griefs,
The bruisings born of broken ties,
All these are steps by which we rise
To living ways of sound beliefs.

Love, pitying, watchful, runs to meet

The Pilgrim from the Land of Fate;
All glory and all good await
The coming of obedient feet.

CHAPTER 4

The Silent Power of Thought: Controlling and Directing One's Forces

The most powerful forces in the universe are the silent forces; and in accordance with the intensity of its power does a force become beneficent when rightly directed and destructive when wrongly employed.

This is a common knowledge in regard to the mechanical forces, such as steam, electricity, etc., but few have yet learned to apply this knowledge to the realm of mind, where the thought-forces (most powerful of all) are continually being generated and sent forth as currents of salvation or destruction.

At this stage of his evolution, man has entered into the possession of these forces, and the whole trend of his present advancement is their complete subjugation. All the wisdom possible to man on this material earth is to be found only in complete self-mastery. The command, "Love your enemies," resolves itself into an exhortation to enter here and now into the possession of that sublime wisdom by taking hold of, mastering, and transmuting those mind forces to which man is now slavishly subject, and by which he is helplessly borne, like a straw on the stream, upon the currents of selfishness.

The Hebrew prophets, with their perfect knowledge of the Supreme Law, always related outward events to inward thought, and associated national disaster or success with the thoughts and desires that dominated the nation at the time.

The knowledge of the causal power of thought is the basis of all their prophecies, as it is the basis of all real wisdom and power. National events are simply the working out of the psychic forces of the nation.

Wars, plagues, and famines are the meeting and clashing of wrongly-directed thought-forces, the culminating points at which destruction steps in as the agent of the Law.

It is foolish to ascribe war to the influence of one person or to one body of people. It is the crowning horror of national selfishness. It is the silent and conquering thought-forces which bring all things into manifestation.

The universe grew out of thought. Matter in its last analysis is found to be merely objectivized thought. All human accomplishments were first wrought out in thought and then objectivized.

The author, the inventor, the architect first builds up their work in thought, and having perfected it in all its parts as a complete and harmonious whole upon the thought-plane, they then commence to materialize it, to bring it down to the material or sense-plane.

When the thought-forces are directed in harmony with the over-ruling Law, they are up-building and preservative, but when subverted they become disintegrating and self-destructive.

To adjust all your thoughts to a perfect and unswerving faith in the omnipotence and supremacy of Good is to co-operate with that Good and to realize within yourself the solution and destruction of all evil. Believe and ye shall live.

And here we have the true meaning of salvation—salvation from the darkness and negation of evil by entering into and realizing the living light of the Eternal Good.

Where there is fear, worry, anxiety, doubt, trouble, chagrin, or disappointment, there is ignorance and lack of faith.

All these conditions of mind are the direct outcome of selfishness, and are based upon an inherent belief in the power and supremacy of evil. They therefore constitute practical atheism; and to live in, and become subject to, these negative and soul-destroying conditions of mind is the only real atheism.

It is salvation from such conditions that the race needs, and let no man boast of salvation while he is their helpless and obedient slave.

To fear or to worry is as sinful as to curse, for how can one fear or worry if he intrinsically believes in the Eternal justice, the Omnipotent Good, the Boundless Love? To fear, to worry, to doubt is to deny, to dis-believe.

It is from such states of mind that all weakness and failure proceed, for they represent the annulling and disintegrating of the positive thought-forces which would otherwise speed to their object with power, and bring about their own beneficent results.

To overcome these negative conditions is to enter into a life of power—is to cease to be a slave and to become a master—and there is only one way by which they can be overcome, and that is by steady and persistent growth in inward knowledge.

To mentally deny evil is not sufficient; it must, by daily practice, be risen above and understood. To mentally affirm the good is inadequate; it must, by unswerving endeavor, be entered into and comprehended.

The intelligent practice of self-control quickly leads to a knowledge of one's interior thought-forces, and, later on, to the acquisition of that power by which they are rightly employed and directed.

In the measure that you master self, that you control your mental forces instead of being controlled by them, in just such measure will you master affairs and outward circumstances.

Show me a man under whose touch everything crumbles away, and who cannot retain success even when it is placed in his hands, and I will show you a man who dwells continually in those conditions of mind which are the very negation of power.

To be forever wallowing in the bogs of doubt, to be drawn continually into the quicksand of fear, or blown ceaselessly about by the winds of anxiety, is to be a slave, and to live the life of a slave, even though success and influence be forever knocking at your door seeking for admittance.

Such a man, being without faith and without self-government, is incapable of the right government of his affairs and is a slave to circumstances—in reality a slave to himself. Such are taught by affliction, and ultimately pass from weakness to strength by the stress of bitter experience. Faith and purpose constitute the motive-power of life.

There is nothing that a strong faith and an unflinching purpose may not accomplish. By the daily exercise of silent faith, the thought-forces are gathered together, and by the daily strengthening of silent purpose, those forces are directed toward the object of accomplishment.

Whatever your position in life may be, before you can hope to enter into any measure of success, usefulness, and power, you must learn how to focus your thought-forces by cultivating calmness and repose. It may be that you are a businessperson, and you are suddenly confronted with some overwhelming difficulty or probable disaster. You grow fearful and anxious and are at your wit's end.

To persist in such a state of mind would be fatal, for when anxiety steps in, correct judgment passes out. Now if you will take advantage of a quiet hour or two in the early morning or at night, and go away to some solitary spot, or to some room in your house where you know you will be absolutely free from intrusion, and, having seated yourself in an easy attitude, you forcibly direct your mind right away from the object of anxiety by dwelling upon something in your life that is pleasing and bliss-giving, a calm, reposeful strength will gradually steal into your mind, and your anxiety will pass away.

Upon the instant that you find your mind reverting to the lower plane of worry, bring it back again and reestablish it on the plane of peace and strength.

When this is fully accomplished, you may then concentrate your whole mind upon the solution of your difficulty, and what was intricate and insurmountable to you in your hour of anxiety will be made plain and easy, and you will see, with that clear vision and perfect judgment which belong only to a calm and untroubled mind, the right course to pursue and the proper end to be brought about.

It may be that you will have to try day after day before you will be able to perfectly calm your mind, but if you persevere you will certainly accomplish it. And the course which is presented to you in that hour of calmness must be carried out.

Doubtless when you are again involved in the business of the day, and worries again creep in and begin to dominate you, you will begin to think that the course is a wrong or foolish one, but do not heed such suggestions.

Be guided absolutely and entirely by the vision of calmness, and not by the shadows of anxiety. The hour of calmness is the hour of illumination and correct judgment.

By such a course of mental discipline, the scattered thought-forces are reunited and directed, like the rays of the searchlight, upon the problem at issue, with the result that it gives way before them.

There is no difficulty, however great, but will yield before a calm and powerful concentration of thought, and no legitimate object but may be speedily actualized by the intelligent use and direction of one's soul-forces.

Not until you have gone deeply and searchingly into your inner nature, and have overcome many enemies that lurk there, can you have any approximate conception of the subtle power of thought, of its inseparable relation to outward and material things, or of its magical potency, when rightly poised and directed, in readjusting and transforming the life-conditions.

Every thought you think is a force sent out, and in accordance with its nature and intensity will it go out to seek a lodgment in minds receptive to it, and will react upon yourself for good or evil. There is ceaseless reciprocity between mind and mind, and a continual interchange of thought-forces.

Selfish and disturbing thoughts are so many malignant and destructive forces, messengers of evil, sent out to stimulate and augment the evil in other minds, which in turn send them back upon you with added power.

While thoughts that are calm, pure, and unselfish are so many angelic messengers sent out into the world with health, healing, and blessedness upon their wings, counteracting the evil forces, pouring the oil of joy upon the troubled waters of anxiety and sorrow, and restoring to broken hearts their heritage of immortality.

Think good thoughts, and they will quickly become actualized in your outward life in the form of good conditions. Control your soul-forces, and you will be able to shape your outward life as you will.

The difference between a savior and a sinner is this—that the one has a perfect control of all the forces within him; the other is dominated and controlled by them.

There is absolutely no other way to true power and abiding peace, but by self-control, self-government, self-purification. To be at the mercy of your disposition is to be impotent, unhappy, and of little real use in the world.

The conquest of your petty likes and dislikes, your capricious loves and hates, your fits of anger, suspicion, jealousy, and all the changing moods to which you are more or less helplessly subject, this is the task you have before you if you would weave into the web of life the golden threads of happiness and prosperity.

In so far as you are enslaved by the changing moods within you, will you need to depend upon others and upon outward aids as you walk through life.

If you would walk firmly and securely, and would accomplish any achievement, you must learn to rise above and control all such disturbing and hindering vibrations.

You must daily practice the habit of putting your mind at rest, "going into the silence," as it is commonly called. This is a method of replacing a troubled thought with one of peace, a thought of weakness with one of strength.

Until you succeed in doing this you cannot hope to direct your mental forces upon the problems and pursuits of life with any appreciable measure of success. It is a process of diverting one's scattered forces into one powerful channel.

Just as a useless marsh may be converted into a field of golden corn or a fruitful garden by draining and directing the scattered and harmful streams into one well-cut channel, so one who acquires calmness and subdues and directs the thought-currents within themselves saves their soul and fructifies their heart and life.

As you succeed in gaining mastery over your impulses and thoughts you will begin to feel, growing up within you, a new and silent power, and a settled feeling of composure and strength will remain with you.

Your latent powers will begin to unfold themselves, and whereas formerly your efforts were weak and ineffectual, you will now be able to work with that calm confidence which commands success.

And along with this new power and strength, there will be awakened within you that interior Illumination known as "intuition," and you will walk no longer in darkness and speculation but in light and certainty.

With the development of this soul-vision, judgment and mental penetration will be incalculably increased, and there will evolve within you that prophetic vision by the aid of which you will be able to sense coming events and to forecast, with remarkable accuracy, the result of your efforts.

And in just the measure that you alter from within will your outlook upon life alter; and as you alter your mental attitude toward others they will alter in their attitude and conduct toward you.

As you rise above the lower, debilitating, and destructive thought-forces, you will come in contact with the positive, strengthening, and up-building currents generated by strong, pure, and noble minds. Your happiness will be immeasurably intensified, and you will begin to realize the joy, strength, and power that are born only of self-mastery.

And this joy, strength, and power will be continually radiating from you, and without any effort on your part, nay, though you are utterly unconscious of it, strong people will be drawn toward you, influence will be put into your hands, and in accordance with your altered thought-world will outward events shape themselves.

"A man's foes are they of his own household," and one who would be useful, strong, and happy must cease to be a passive receptacle for the negative, beggardly, and impure streams of thought. As a wise householder commands his servants and invites his guests, so must he learn to command his desires, and to say, with authority, what thoughts he shall admit into the mansion of his soul.

Even a very partial success in self-mastery adds greatly to one's power, and one who succeeds in perfecting this divine accomplishment enters into possession of undreamed-of wisdom and inward strength and peace, and realizes that all the forces of the universe aid and protect the footsteps of one who is master of his soul.

Would you scale the highest heaven,
Would you pierce the lowest hell,
Live in dreams of constant beauty,
Or in basest thinkings dwell.

For your thoughts are heaven above you,
And your thoughts are hell below,
Bliss is not, except in thinking,
Torment nought but thought can know.

Worlds would vanish but for thinking;
Glory is not but in dreams;
And the Drama of the ages
From the Thought Eternal streams.

Dignity and shame and sorrow,

Pain and anguish, love and hate
Are but maskings of the mighty
Pulsing Thought that governs Fate.

As the colors of the rainbow
Makes the one uncolored beam,
So the universal changes
Make the One Eternal Dream.

And the Dream is all within you,
And the Dreamer waiteth long
For the Morning to awake him
To the living thought and strong.

That shall make the ideal real,
Make to vanish dreams of hell
In the highest, holiest heaven
Where the pure and perfect dwell.

Evil is the thought that thinks it;
Good, the thought that makes it so
Light and darkness, sin and pureness
Likewise out of thinking grow.

Dwell in thought upon the Grandest,
And the Grandest you shall see ;
Fix your mind upon the Highest,
And the Highest you shall be.

CHAPTER 5

The Secret of Health, Success, and Power

We all remember with what intense delight, as children, we listened to the never-tiring fairytale. How eagerly we followed the fluctuating fortunes of the good boy or girl, ever protected, in the hour of crisis, from the evil machinations of the scheming witch, the cruel giant, or the wicked king.

And our little hearts never faltered for the fate of the hero or heroine, nor did we doubt their ultimate triumph over all their enemies, for we knew that the fairies were infallible, and that they would never desert those who had consecrated themselves to the good and the true.

And what unspeakable joy pulsated within us when the Fairy Queen, bringing all her magic to bear at the critical moment, scattered all the darkness and trouble, and granted them the complete satisfaction of all their hopes, and they were "happy ever after."

With the accumulating years and an ever-increasing intimacy with the so-called "realities" of life, our beautiful fairy-world became obliterated, and its wonderful inhabitants were relegated, in the archives of memory, to the shadowy and unreal.

And we thought we were wise and strong in thus leaving forever the land of childish dreams, but as we re-become little children in the wondrous world of wisdom, we shall return again to the inspiring dreams of childhood and find that they are, after all, realities.

The fairy-folk, so small and nearly always invisible, yet possessed of an all-conquering and magical power, who bestow upon the good health, wealth, and happiness, along with all the gifts of nature in lavish profusion, start again into reality and become immortalized in the soul-realm of one who, by growth in wisdom, has entered into a knowledge of the power of thought and the laws which govern the inner world of being.

To them, the fairies live again as thought-people, thought-messengers, thought-powers working in harmony with the over-ruling Good. And they who, day by day, endeavor to harmonize their hearts with the heart of the Supreme Good, do in reality acquire true health, wealth, and happiness.

There is no protection to compare with goodness, and by "goodness" I do not mean a mere outward conformity to the rules of morality; I mean pure thought, noble aspiration, unselfish love, and freedom from vainglory.

To dwell continually in good thoughts is to throw around oneself a psychic atmosphere of sweetness and power which leaves its impress upon all who come in contact with it.

As the rising sun puts to rout the helpless shadows, so are all the impotent forces of evil put to flight by the searching rays of positive thought which shine forth from a heart made strong in purity and faith.

Where there is sterling faith and uncompromising purity there is health, there is success, there is power. In such a one, disease, failure, and disaster can find no lodgment, for there is nothing on which they can feed.

Even physical conditions are largely determined by mental states, and to this truth the scientific world is rapidly being drawn.

The old, materialistic belief that a person is what their body makes them is rapidly passing away and is being replaced by the inspiring belief that people are superior to their bodies and that their bodies are what they make them by the power of thought.

People everywhere are ceasing to believe that a person is despairing because they are dyspeptic, and are coming to understand that they are dyspeptic because they are despairing. In the near future, the fact that all disease has its origin in the mind will become common knowledge.

There is no evil in the universe but has its root and origin in the mind, and sin, sickness, sorrow, and affliction do not, in reality, belong to the universal order, are not inherent in the nature of things, but are the direct outcome of our ignorance of the right relations of things.

According to tradition, there once lived, in India, a school of philosophers who led a life of such absolute purity and simplicity that they commonly reached the age of one hundred and fifty years, and to fall sick was looked upon by them as an unpardonable disgrace, for it was considered to indicate a violation of law.

The sooner we realize and acknowledge that sickness, far from being the arbitrary visitation of an offended God or the test of an unwise Providence, is the result of our own error or sin, the sooner shall we enter upon the highway of health.

Disease comes to those who attract it, to those whose minds and bodies are receptive to it, and flees from those whose strong, pure, and positive thought-sphere generates healing and life-giving currents.

If you are given to anger, worry, jealousy, greed, or any other inharmonious state of mind and expect perfect physical health, you are expecting the impossible, for you are continually sowing the seeds of disease in your mind.

Such conditions of mind are carefully shunned by the wise person, for they know them to be far more dangerous than a bad drain or an infected house.

If you would be free from all physical aches and pains, and would enjoy perfect physical harmony, then put your mind in order and harmonize your thoughts. Think joyful thoughts; think loving thoughts; let the elixir of goodwill course through your veins, and you will need no other medicine. Put away your jealousies, your suspicions, your worries, your hatreds, your selfish indulgences, and you will put away your dyspepsia, your biliousness, your nervousness and aching joints.

If you will persist in clinging to these debilitating and demoralizing habits of mind, then do not complain when your body is laid low with sickness. The following story illustrates the close relation that exists between habits of mind and bodily conditions.

A certain man was afflicted with a painful disease, and he tried one physician after another, but all to no purpose. He then visited towns which were famous for their curative waters, and after having bathed in them all, his disease was more painful than ever.

One night he dreamed that a Presence came to him and said, "Brother, hast thou tried all the means of cure?" and he replied, "I have tried all." "Nay," said the Presence, "Come with me, and I will show thee a healing bath which has escaped thy notice."

The afflicted man followed, and the Presence led him to a clear pool of water, and said, "Plunge thyself in this water and thou shalt surely recover," and thereupon vanished.

The man plunged into the water, and on coming out, lo! his disease had left him, and at the same moment he saw written above the pool the word "Renounce." Upon waking, the full meaning of his dream flashed across his mind, and looking within he discovered that he had, all along, been a victim to a sinful indulgence, and he vowed that he would renounce it forever.

He carried out his vow, and from that day his affliction began to leave him, and in a short time he was completely restored to health. Many people complain that they have broken down through over-work. In the majority of such cases the breakdown is more frequently the result of foolishly wasted energy.

If you would secure health you must learn to work without friction. To become anxious or excited or to worry over needless details is to invite a breakdown.

Work, whether of brain or body, is beneficial and health-giving, and the man who can work with a steady and calm persistency, freed from all anxiety and worry, and with his mind utterly oblivious to all but the work he has in hand, will not only accomplish far more than the man who is always hurried and anxious, but he will retain his health, a boon which the other quickly forfeits.

True health and true success go together, for they are inseparably intertwined in the thought-realm. As mental harmony produces bodily health, so it also leads to a harmonious sequence in the actual working out of one's plans.

Order your thoughts and you will order your life. Pour the oil of tranquility upon the turbulent waters of the passions and prejudices, and the tempests of misfortune, howsoever they may threaten, will be powerless to wreck the ship of your soul as it threads its way across the ocean of life.

And if that ship be piloted by a cheerful and never-failing faith, its course will be doubly sure, and many perils will pass it by which would otherwise attack it.

By the power of faith every enduring work is accomplished. Faith in the Supreme; faith in the over-ruling Law; faith in your work, and in your power to accomplish that work—here is the rock upon which you must build if you would achieve, if you would stand and not fall.

To follow, under all circumstances, the highest promptings within you; to be always true to the divine self; to rely upon the inward Light, the inward Voice, and to pursue your purpose with a fearless and restful heart, believing that the future will yield unto you the mead of every thought and effort; knowing that the laws of the universe can never fail, and that your own will come back to you with mathematical exactitude—this is faith and the living of faith.

By the power of such a faith the dark waters of uncertainty are divided, every mountain of difficulty crumbles away, and the believing soul passes on unharmed.

Strive, O reader, to acquire, above everything, the priceless possession of this dauntless faith, for it is the talisman of happiness, of success, of peace, of power, of all that makes life great and superior to suffering.

Build upon such a faith, and you build upon the Rock of the Eternal and with the materials of the Eternal, and the structure that you erect will never be dissolved, for it will transcend all the accumulations of material luxuries and riches, the end of which is dust.

Whether you are hurled into the depths of sorrow or lifted upon the heights of joy, ever retain your hold upon this faith, ever return to it as your rock of refuge, and keep your feet firmly planted upon its immortal and immovable base.

Centered in such a faith, you will become possessed of such a spiritual strength as will shatter, like so many toys of glass, all the forces of evil that are hurled against you, and you will achieve a success such as the mere striver after worldly gain can never know or even dream of. "If ye have faith, and doubt not, ye shall not only do this...but if ye shall say unto this mountain, be thou removed and be thou cast into the sea, it shall be done."

There are those today, men and women tabernacled in flesh and blood, who have realized this faith, who live in it and by it day by day, and who, having put it to the uttermost test, have entered into the possession of its glory and peace.

Such have sent out the word of command, and the mountains of sorrow and disappointment, of mental weariness and physical pain have passed from them and have been cast into the sea of oblivion.

If you will become possessed of this faith you will not need to trouble about your success or failure, and success will come.

You will not need to become anxious about results, but will work joyfully and peacefully, knowing that right thoughts and right efforts will inevitably bring about right results.

I know a lady who has entered into many blissful satisfactions, and recently a friend remarked to her, "Oh, how fortunate you are! You only have to wish for a thing, and it comes to you."

And it did, indeed, appear so on the surface; but in reality all the blessedness that has entered into this woman's life is the direct outcome of the inward state of blessedness which she has, throughout life, been cultivating and training toward perfection.

Mere wishing brings nothing but disappointment; it is living that tells.

The foolish wish and grumble; the wise work and wait. And this woman had worked—worked without and within, but especially within upon heart and soul—and with the invisible hands of the spirit she had built up, with the precious stones of faith, hope, joy, devotion, and love, a fair temple of light, whose glorifying radiance was ever round about her.

It beamed in her eye; it shone through her countenance; it vibrated in her voice; and all who came into her presence felt its captivating spell.

And as with her, so with you. Your success, your failure, your influence, your whole life you carry about with you, for your dominant trends of thought are the determining factors in your destiny.

Send forth loving, stainless, and happy thoughts, and blessings will fall into your hands, and your table will be spread with the cloth of peace.

Send forth hateful, impure, and unhappy thoughts, and curses will rain down upon you, and fear and unrest will wait upon your pillow. You are the unconditional maker of your fate, be that fate what it may. Every moment you are sending forth from you the influences which will make or mar your life.

Let your heart grow large and loving and unselfish, and great and lasting will be your influence and success, even though you make little money.

Confine it within the narrow limits of self-interest, and even though you become a millionaire your influence and success, at the final reckoning, will be found to be utterly insignificant. Cultivate, then, this pure and unselfish spirit, and combine with purity and faith, singleness of purpose, and you are evolving from within the elements, not only of abounding health and enduring success, but of greatness and power.

If your present position is distasteful to you, and your heart is not in your work, nevertheless perform your duties with scrupulous diligence, and while resting your mind in the idea that the better position and greater opportunities are waiting for you, ever keep an active mental outlook for budding possibilities, so that when the critical moment arrives and the new channel presents itself, you will step into it with your mind fully prepared for the undertaking, and with that intelligence and foresight which is born of mental discipline.

Whatever your task may be, concentrate your whole mind upon it, throw into it all the energy of which you are capable. The faultless completion of small tasks leads inevitably to larger tasks. See to it that you rise by steady climbing, and you will never fall. And herein lies the secret of true power.

Learn, by constant practice, how to husband your resources, and to concentrate them, at any moment, upon a given point. The foolish waste all their mental and spiritual energy in frivolity, foolish chatter, or selfish argument, not to mention wasteful physical excesses.

If you would acquire overcoming power you must cultivate poise and passivity. You must be able to stand alone. All power is associated with immovability. The mountain, the massive rock, the storm-tried oak—all speak to us of power, because of their combined solitary grandeur and defiant fixity; while the shifting sand, the yielding twig, and the waving reed speak to us of weakness, because they are movable and non-resistant, and are utterly useless when detached from their fellows.

He is the man of power who, when all his fellows are swayed by some emotion or passion, remains calm and unmoved. He only is fitted to command and control who has succeeded in commanding and controlling himself.

The hysterical, the fearful, the thoughtless and frivolous—let such seek company, or they will fall for lack of support. But the calm, the fearless, the thoughtful—let such seek the solitude of the forest, the desert, and the mountain-top, and to their power more power will be added, and they will more and more successfully stem the psychic currents and whirlpools which engulf humankind.

Passion is not power; it is the abuse of power, the dispersion of power. Passion is like a furious storm which beats fiercely and wildly upon the embattled rock while power is like the rock itself, which remains silent and unmoved through it all.

That was a manifestation of true power when Martin Luther, wearied with the persuasions of his fearful friends, who were doubtful as to his safety should he go to Worms, replied, "If there were as many devils in Worms as there are tiles on the housetops I would go."

And when Benjamin Disraeli broke down in his first Parliamentary speech and brought upon himself the derision of the House, that was an exhibition of germinal power when he exclaimed, "The day will come when you will consider it an honor to listen to me."

When that young man, whom I knew, passing through continual reverses and misfortunes, was mocked by his friends and told to desist from further effort, and he replied, "The time is not far distant when you will marvel at my good fortune and success," he showed that he was possessed of that silent and irresistible power which has taken him over innumerable difficulties and crowned his life with success.

If you have not this power, you may acquire it by practice, and the beginning of power is likewise the beginning of wisdom. You must commence by overcoming those purposeless trivialities to which you have hitherto been a willing victim.

Boisterous and uncontrolled laughter, slander and idle talk, and joking merely to raise a laugh, all these things must be put on one side as so much waste of valuable energy.

St. Paul never showed his wonderful insight into the hidden laws of human progress to greater advantage than when he warned the Ephesians against "Foolish talking and jesting which is not convenient," for to dwell habitually in such practices is to destroy all spiritual power and life.

As you succeed in rendering yourself impervious to such mental dissipations you will begin to understand what true power is, and you will then commence to grapple with the more powerful desires and appetites which hold your soul in bondage and bar the way to power, and your further progress will then be made clear.

Above all be of single aim; have a legitimate and useful purpose, and devote yourself unreservedly to it. Let nothing draw you aside; remember that the doubleminded man is unstable in all his ways.

Be eager to learn, but slow to beg. Have a thorough understanding of your work, and let it be your own; and as you proceed, ever following the inward Guide, the infallible Voice, you will pass on from victory to victory and will rise step by step to higher resting-places, and your ever-broadening outlook will gradually reveal to you the essential beauty and purpose of life.

Self-purified, health will be yours; faith-protected, success will be yours; self-governed, power will be yours, and all that you do will prosper, for, ceasing to be a disjointed unit, self-enslaved, you will be in harmony with the Great Law, working no longer against but with the Universal Life, the Eternal Good.

And what health you gain it will remain with you; what success you achieve will be beyond all human computation, and will never pass away; and what influence and power you wield will continue to increase throughout the ages, for it will be a part of that unchangeable Principle which supports the universe.

This, then, is the secret of health—a pure heart and a well-ordered mind. This is the secret of success—an unfaltering faith and a wisely-directed purpose; and to rein in, with unfaltering will, the dark steed of desire, this is the secret of power.

All ways are waiting for my feet to tread,
The light and dark, the living and the dead,
The broad and narrow way, the high and low,
The good and bad, and with quick step or slow,
I now may enter any way I will,
And find, by walking, which is good, which ill.

And all good things my wandering feet await,
If I but come, with vow inviolate,
Unto the narrow, high and holy way
Of heart-born purity, and therein stay;
Walking, secure from him who taunts and scorns,
To flowery meads, across the path of thorns.

And I may stand where health, success, and power
Await my coming, if, each fleeting hour,
I cling to love and patience; and abide
With stainlessness; and never step aside

From high integrity; so shall I see
At last the land of immortality.

And I may seek and find; I may achieve,
I may not claim, but, losing, may retrieve.
The law bends not for me, but I must bend
Unto the law, if I would reach the end
Of my afflictions, if I would restore
My soul to Light and Life, and weep no more.

Not mine the arrogant and selfish claim
To all good things; be mine the lowly aim
To seek and find, to know and comprehend,
And wisdom-ward all holy footsteps wend,
Nothing is mine to claim or to command,
But all is mine to know and understand.

CHAPTER 6

The Secret of Abounding Happiness

Great is the thirst for happiness, and equally great is the lack of happiness. The majority of the poor long for riches, believing that their possession would bring them supreme and lasting happiness. Many who are rich, having gratified every desire and whim, suffer from ennui and repletion and are further from the possession of happiness even than the very poor.

If we reflect upon this state of things it will ultimately lead us to a knowledge of the all-important truth that happiness is not derived from mere outward possessions, nor misery from the lack of them; for if this were so, we should find the poor always miserable, and the rich always happy, whereas the reverse is frequently the case.

Some of the most wretched people whom I have known were those who were surrounded with riches and luxury, while some of the brightest and happiest people I have met were possessed of only the barest necessities of life.

Many people who have accumulated riches have confessed that the selfish gratification which followed the acquisition of riches has robbed life of its sweetness, and that they were never so happy as when they were poor.

What, then, is happiness, and how is it to be secured? Is it a figment, a delusion, and is suffering alone perennial? We shall find, after earnest observation and reflection, that all, except those who have entered the way of wisdom, believe that happiness is only to be obtained by the gratification of desire.

It is this belief, rooted in the soil of ignorance and continually watered by selfish cravings, that is the cause of all the misery in the world.

And I do not limit the word *desire* to the grosser animal cravings; it extends to the higher psychic realm, where far more powerful, subtle, and insidious cravings hold in bondage the intellectual and refined, depriving them of all that beauty, harmony, and purity of soul whose expression is happiness.

Most people will admit that selfishness is the cause of all the unhappiness in the world, but they fall under the soul-destroying delusion that it is somebody else's selfishness and not their own.

When you are willing to admit that all your unhappiness is the result of your own selfishness you will not be far from the gates of Paradise; but so long as you are convinced that it is the selfishness of others that is robbing you of joy, so long will you remain a prisoner in your self-created purgatory.

Happiness is that inward state of perfect satisfaction which is joy and peace and from which all desire is eliminated. The satisfaction which results from gratified desire is brief and illusionary and is always followed by an increased demand for gratification.

Desire is as insatiable as the ocean and clamors louder and louder as its demands are attended to.

It claims ever-increasing service from its deluded devotees, until at last they are struck down with physical or mental anguish and are hurled into the purifying fires of suffering. Desire is the region of hell, and all torments are centered there.

The giving up of desire is the realization of heaven, and all delights await the pilgrim there:

I sent my soul through the invisible,
Some letter of that after life to spell,
And by-and-by my soul returned to me,
And whispered, "I myself am heaven and hell."

Heaven and hell are inward states. Sink into self and all its gratifications, and you sink into hell; rise above self into that state of consciousness which is the utter denial and forgetfulness of self, and you enter heaven.

Self is blind, without judgment, not possessed of true knowledge, and always leads to suffering. Correct perception, unbiased judgment, and true knowledge belong only to the divine state, and only in so far as you realize this divine consciousness can you know what real happiness is.

So long as you persist in selfishly seeking for your own personal happiness, so long will happiness elude you, and you will be sowing the seeds of wretchedness.

In so far as you succeed in losing yourself in the service of others, in that measure will happiness come to you, and you will reap a harvest of bliss.

It is in loving, not in being loved,
The heart is blessed;

It is in giving, not in seeking gifts,
We find our quest.

Whatever be thy longing or thy need,
That do thou give;
So shall thy soul be fed, and thou indeed
Shalt truly live.

Cling to self, and you cling to sorrow; relinquish self, and you enter into peace. To seek selfishly is not only to lose happiness, but even that which we believe to be the source of happiness.

See how the glutton is continually looking about for a new delicacy wherewith to stimulate his deadened appetite; and how, bloated, burdened, and diseased, scarcely any food at last is eaten with pleasure.

Whereas, one who has mastered their appetite, and not only does not seek, but never thinks of gustatory pleasure, finds delight in the most frugal meal. The angel-form of happiness, which people, looking through the eyes of self, imagine they see in gratified desire, when clasped is always found to be the skeleton of misery. Truly, "He that seeketh his life shall lose it, and he that loseth his life shall find it."

Abiding happiness will come to you when, ceasing to selfishly cling, you are willing to give up. When you are willing to lose, unreservedly, that impermanent thing which is so dear to you, and which, whether you cling to it or not, will one day be snatched from you, then you will find that that which seemed to you like a painful loss turns out to be a supreme gain.

To give up in order to gain—than this there is no greater delusion, nor no more prolific source of misery; but to be willing to yield up and to suffer loss, this is indeed the Way of Life.

How is it possible to find real happiness by centering ourselves in those things which, by their very nature, must pass away? Abiding and real happiness can only be found by centering ourselves in that which is permanent.

Rise, therefore, above the clinging to and the craving for impermanent things, and you will then enter into a consciousness of the Eternal, and as, rising above self, and by growing more and more into the spirit of purity, self-sacrifice and universal Love, you become centered in that consciousness, you will realize that happiness which has no reaction and which can never be taken from you.

The heart that has reached utter self-forgetfulness in its love for others has not only become possessed of the highest happiness but has entered into immortality, for it has realized the Divine.

Look back upon your life, and you will find that the moments of supremest happiness were those in which you uttered some word or performed some act of compassion or self-denying love. Spiritually, happiness and harmony are synonymous.

Harmony is one phase of the Great Law whose spiritual expression is love. All selfishness is discord, and to be selfish is to be out of harmony with the Divine order.

As we realize that all-embracing love which is the negation of self, we put ourselves in harmony with the divine music, the universal song, and that ineffable melody which is true happiness becomes our own.

Men and women are rushing hither and thither in the blind search for happiness, and cannot find it; nor ever will until they recognize that happiness is already within them and round about them, filling the universe, and that they in their selfish searching are shutting themselves out from it.

I followed happiness to make her mine,
Past towering oak and swinging ivy vine.
She fled, I chased, o'er slanting hill and dale,

O'er fields and meadows, in the purpling vale;
Pursuing rapidly o'er dashing stream.
I scaled the dizzy cliffs where eagles scream;
I traversed swiftly every land and sea,
But always happiness eluded me.

Exhausted, fainting, I pursued no more,
But sank to rest upon a barren shore.
One came and asked for food, and one for alms
I placed the bread and gold in bony palms.
One came for sympathy, and one for rest;
I shared with every needy one my best;
When, lo! sweet Happiness, with form divine,
Stood by me, whispering softly, "I am thine."

These beautiful lines of Burleigh's express the secret of all abounding happiness. Sacrifice the personal and transient, and you rise at once into the impersonal and permanent.

Give up that narrow, cramped self that seeks to render all things subservient to its own petty interests, and you will enter into the company of the angels, into the very heart and essence of universal Love.

Forget yourself entirely in the sorrows of others and in ministering to others, and divine happiness will emancipate you from all sorrow and suffering.

"Taking the first step with a good thought, the second with a good word, and the third with a good deed, I entered Paradise." And you also may enter into Paradise by pursuing the same course. It is not beyond, it is here. It is realized only by the unselfish.

It is known in its fullness only to the pure in heart. If you have not realized this unbounded happiness you may begin to actualize it by ever holding before you the lofty ideal of unselfish love and aspiring toward it.

Aspiration or prayer is desire turned upward. It is the soul turning toward its Divine source, where alone permanent satisfaction can be found. By aspiration the destructive forces of desire are transmuted into divine and all-preserving energy.

To aspire is to make an effort to shake off the trammels of desire; it is the prodigal made wise by loneliness and suffering, returning to his Father's Mansion.

As you rise above the sordid self; as you break, one after another, the chains that bind you, will you realize the joy of giving, as distinguished from the misery of grasping—giving of your substance, giving of your intellect, giving of the love and light that is growing within you.

You will then understand that it is indeed "more blessed to give than to receive." But the giving must be of the heart without any taint of self, without desire for reward. The gift of pure love is always attended with bliss. If, after you have given, you are wounded because you are not thanked or flattered or your name put in the paper, know then that your gift was prompted by vanity and not by love, and you were merely giving in order to get—you were not really giving but grasping.

Lose yourself in the welfare of others; forget yourself in all that you do; this is the secret of abounding happiness.

Ever be on the watch to guard against selfishness, and learn faithfully the divine lessons of inward sacrifice; so shall you climb the highest heights of happiness and shall remain in the never-clouded sunshine of universal joy, clothed in the shining garment of immortality.

Are you searching for the happiness that does not fade away?
Are you looking for the joy that lives, and leaves no grievous day?
Are you panting for the water-brooks of Love, and Life, and Peace?
Then let all dark desires depart,

and selfish seeking cease.

Are you ling'ring in the paths of pain, grief-haunted,
stricken sore?
Are you wand'ring in the ways that wound your
weary feet the more?
Are you sighing for the Resting-Place where tears
and sorrows cease?
Then sacrifice your selfish heart
and find the Heart of Peace.

CHAPTER 7

The Realization of Prosperity

It is granted only to the heart that abounds with integrity, trust, generosity, and love to realize true prosperity. The heart that is not possessed of these qualities cannot know prosperity, for prosperity, like happiness, is not an outward possession, but an inward realization.

The greedy person may become a millionaire, but they will always be wretched, and mean, and poor, and will even consider themselves outwardly poor so long as there is a person in the world who is richer than they; while the upright, the open-handed and loving will realize a full and rich prosperity, even though their outward possessions may be small.

He is poor who is dissatisfied; he is rich who is contented with what he has, and he is richer who is generous with what he has.

When we contemplate the fact that the universe is abounding in all good things, material as well as spiritual, and compare it with man's blind eagerness to secure a few gold coins, or a few acres of dirt, it is then that we realize how dark and ignorant selfishness is; it is then that we know that self-seeking is self-destruction.

Nature gives all, without reservation, and loses nothing; man, grasping all, loses everything.

If you would realize true prosperity do not settle down, as many have done, into the belief that if you do right everything will go wrong. Do not allow the word "competition" to shake your faith in the supremacy of righteousness.

I care not what men may say about the "laws of competition," for do I not know the unchangeable Law, which shall one day put them all to rout, and which puts them to rout even now in the heart and life of the righteous man?

And knowing this Law I can contemplate all dishonesty with undisturbed repose, for I know where certain destruction awaits it. Under all circumstances do that which you believe to be right, and trust the Law; trust the Divine Power that is imminent in the universe, and it will never desert you, and you will always be protected.

By such a trust all your losses will be converted into gains, and all curses which threaten will be transmuted into blessings. Never let go of integrity, generosity, and love, for these, coupled with energy, will lift you into the truly prosperous state.

Do not believe the world when it tells you that you must always attend to "number one" first, and to others afterward. To do this is not to think of others at all, but only of one's own comforts.

To those who practice this the day will come when they will be deserted by all, and when they cry out in their loneliness and anguish there will be no one to hear and help them. To consider one's self before all others is to cramp and warp and hinder every noble and divine impulse.

Let your soul expand, let your heart reach out to others in loving and generous warmth, and great and lasting will be your joy, and all prosperity will come to you. Those who have wandered from the highway of righteousness guard themselves against competition; those who always pursue the right need not to trouble about such defense.

This is no empty statement. There are many today who, by the power of integrity and faith, have defied all competition, and who, without swerving in the least from their methods, when competed with, have risen steadily into prosperity, while those who tried to undermine them have fallen back defeated.

To possess those inward qualities which constitute goodness is to be armored against all the powers of evil, and to be doubly protected in every time of trial; and to build oneself up in those qualities is to build up a success which cannot be shaken, and to enter into a prosperity which will endure forever.

The White Robe of the Heart Invisible
Is stained with sin and sorrow, grief and pain,
And all repentant pools and springs of prayer
Shall not avail to wash it white again.

While in the path of ignorance I walk,
The stains of error will not cease to cling
Defilements mark the crooked path of self,
Where anguish lurks and disappointments sting.

Knowledge and wisdom only can avail
To purify and make my garment clean,
For therein lie love's waters; therein rests
Peace undisturbed, eternal, and serene.

Sin and repentance is the path of pain,
Knowledge and wisdom is the path of Peace

By the near way of practice I will find
Where bliss begins, how pains and sorrows cease.

Self shall depart, and Truth shall take its place
The Changeless One, the Indivisible
Shall take up His abode in me, and cleanse
The White Robe of the Heart Invisible.

About James Allen

James Allen (1864–1912) was a British philosophical writer and pioneer of the self-help movement known for his inspirational books and poetry. His best known work, *As a Man Thinketh*, has been mass-produced since its publication in 1902. It has been a source of inspiration to motivational and self-help authors. In 1902, Allen began to publish his own spiritual magazine, *The Light of Reason*, later retitled *The Epoch*.

In 1903, the Allen family retired to the town of Ilfracombe where Allen would spend the rest of his life. Continuing to publish *The Epoch*, Allen wrote nineteen books in nine years, until his death in 1912. Following his death, his wife continued publishing his magazine, *The Epoch*.

THANK YOU FOR READING THIS BOOK!

If you found any of the information helpful, please take a few minutes and leave a review on the bookselling platform of your choice.

BONUS GIFT!

Don't forget to sign up to try our newsletter and grab your free personal development ebook here:

soundwisdom.com/classics